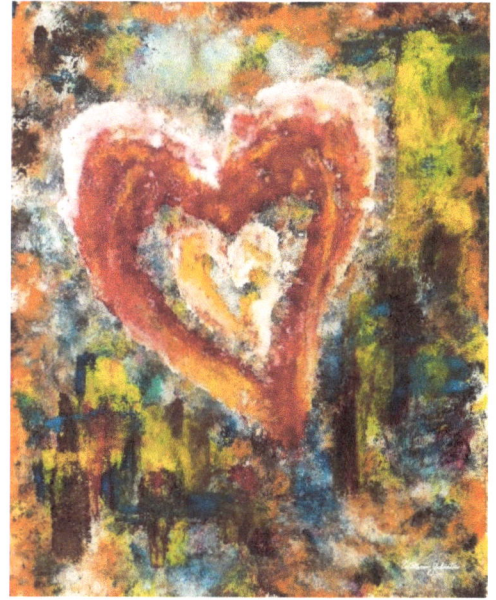

'The Invitation'
by William Johnston

The Seeds of His Love

You will be amazed and inspired when you contemplate *The Seeds of His Love*. These paintings were done under the inspiration of His generosity and are intended to edify the viewer and bring about a better understanding of who The Divine Father is as told to us from *His Holy Word*. The answer to the question, "How can I sow the Seeds of His Love?" is neither simple nor is it difficult; it is a process. It can be found in our journey from earth to heaven in that we are all pilgrims and it is a long walk from earth to heaven. Discover the everlasting love and forgiveness of your Heavenly Father and be guided into a deep and genuine relationship with Him as you explore *The Seeds of His Love.*

This book of paintings and scripture is painted from the heart. Some paintings will seem more difficult than others to understand, so find a quiet time and experience a journey into the mind and heart of the Almighty. These oil paintings are your friend and companion; they were painted for you. They will help you discover the very nature of your Heavenly Father and experience His almighty everlasting love.

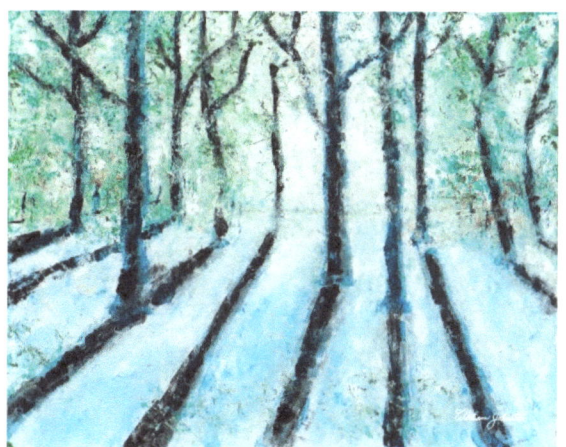

'He will show you the way'
by artist William Johnston

The Sower of His Love

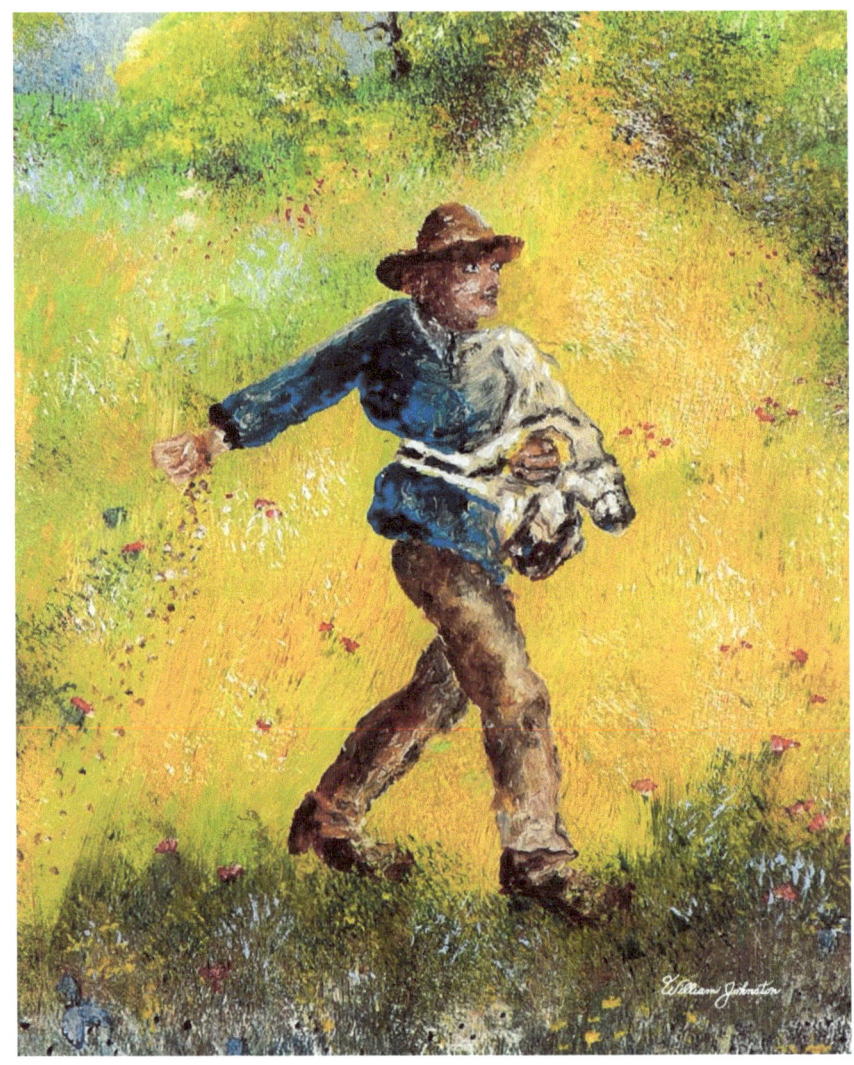

The Sower by artist William Johnston

ISBN-13: 978-1495935459
ISBN-10: 1495935450

Seventh Printing January 2016

The Harvest

It is beautiful watching the green stems of wheat turn golden and then tipping their heads toward the earth as if giving thanks to God. Sowing the seed of God's Love into the landscape of the human mind brings a harvest made in heaven where the angels sing for joy as confessions are made and believers come to know the saving grace of the Lord. "The harvest is plentiful but the laborers are few.' Matthew 9:37

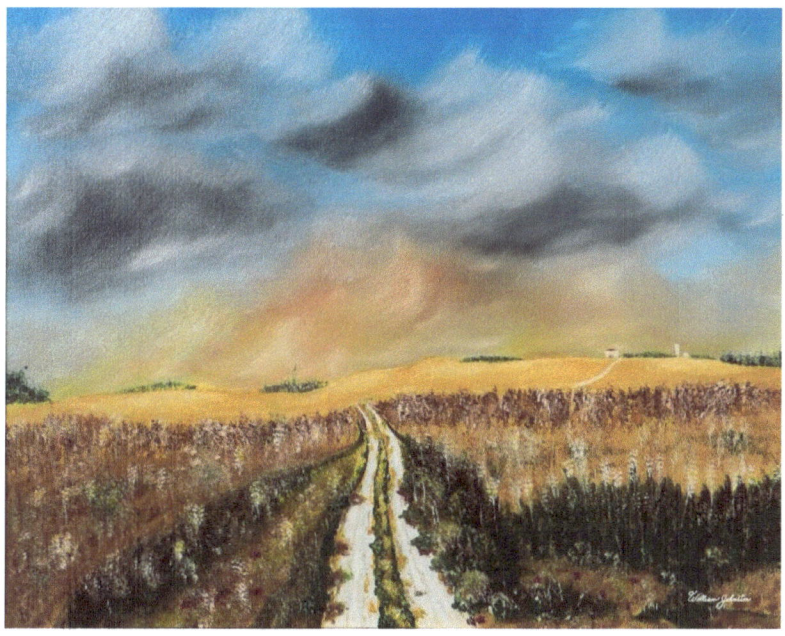

The Harvest by artist William Johnston

Welcome to the Church in the valley. Come on in, the doors are open and the lights are on. A place has been reserved just for you. He's been waiting.

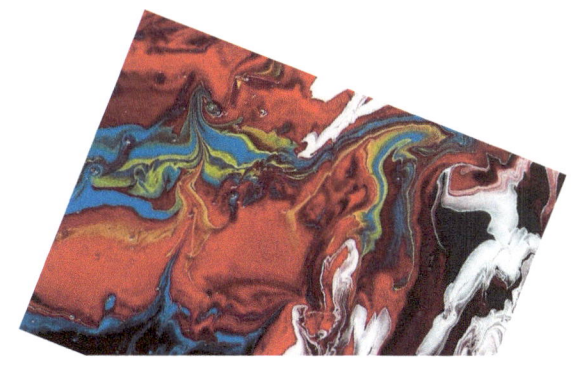

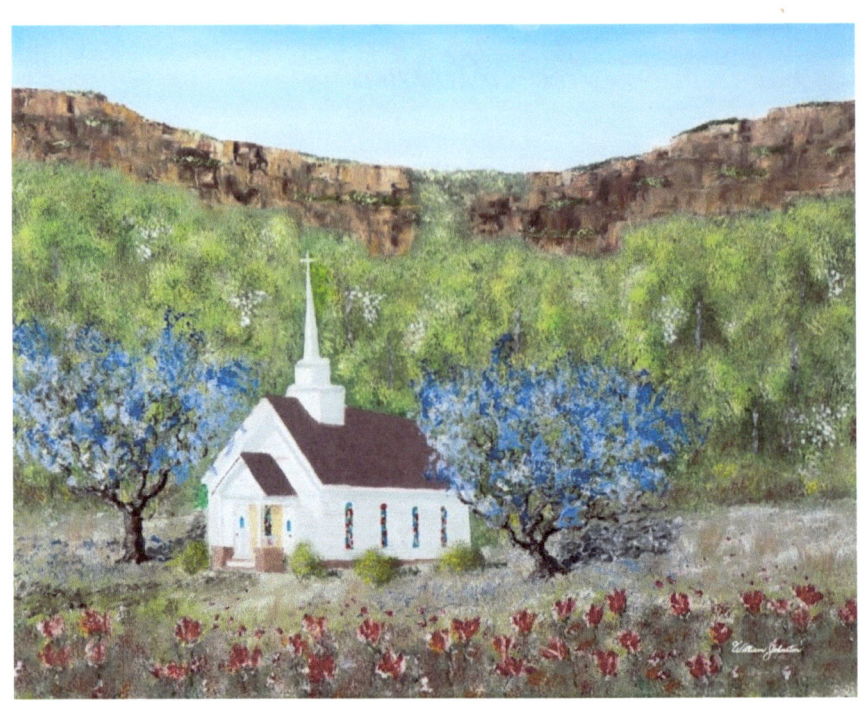

Amazing Grace, how sweet the sound, that saved a wretch like me....

I once was lost but now am found, was blind, but now, I see.

John Newton (1725-1807)

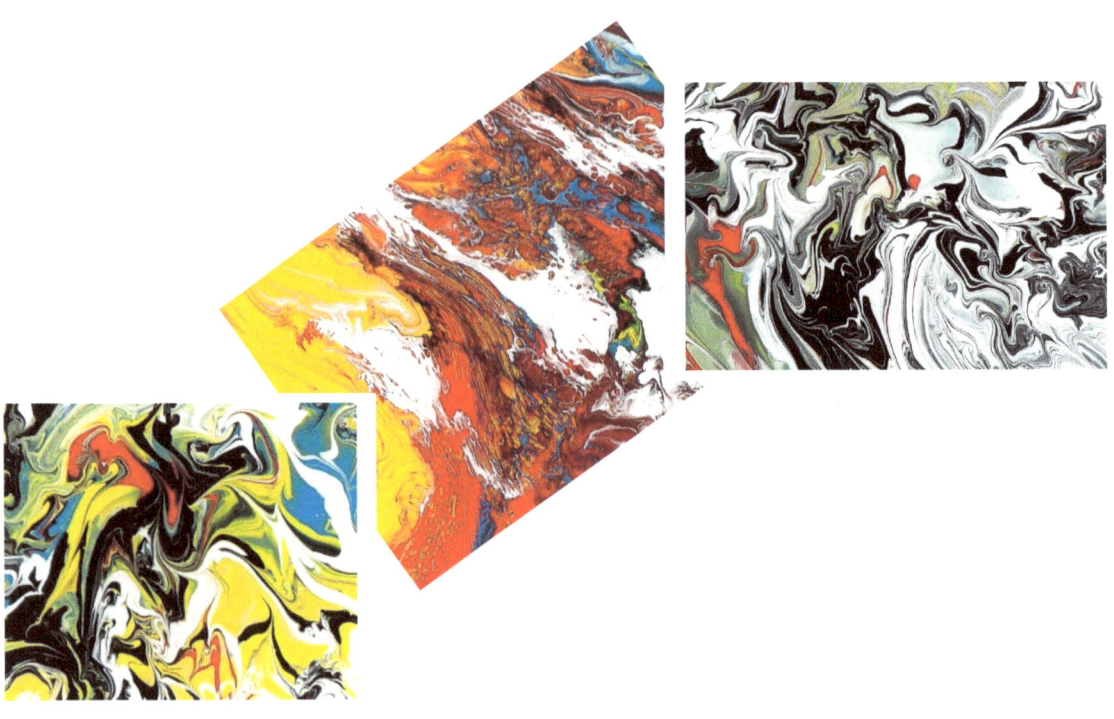

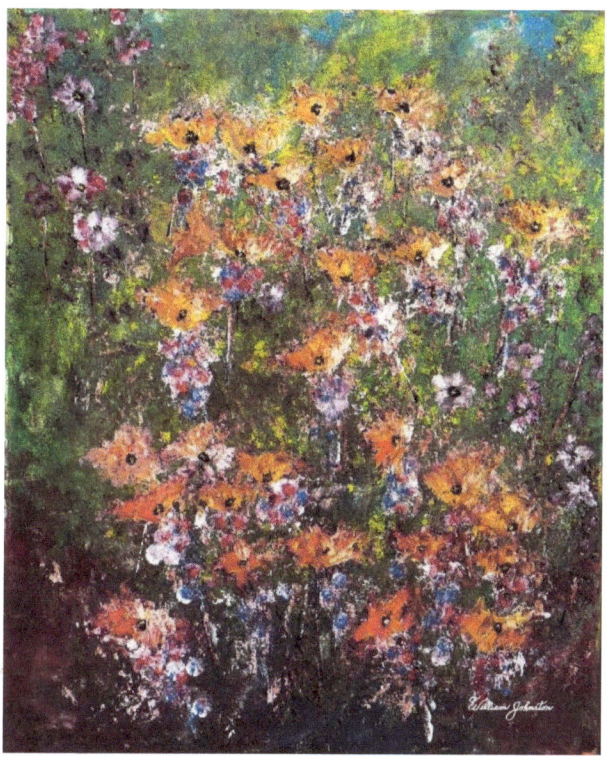

The Fire of Faith is kindled this day by the flowers so softly given, to teach the heart to be a part of a spirit never broken. The Fire of Faith guides this hand so lovingly touched with colors bright, so when in need reach out and touch the Fire of Faith given as He has spoken.

By William Johnston

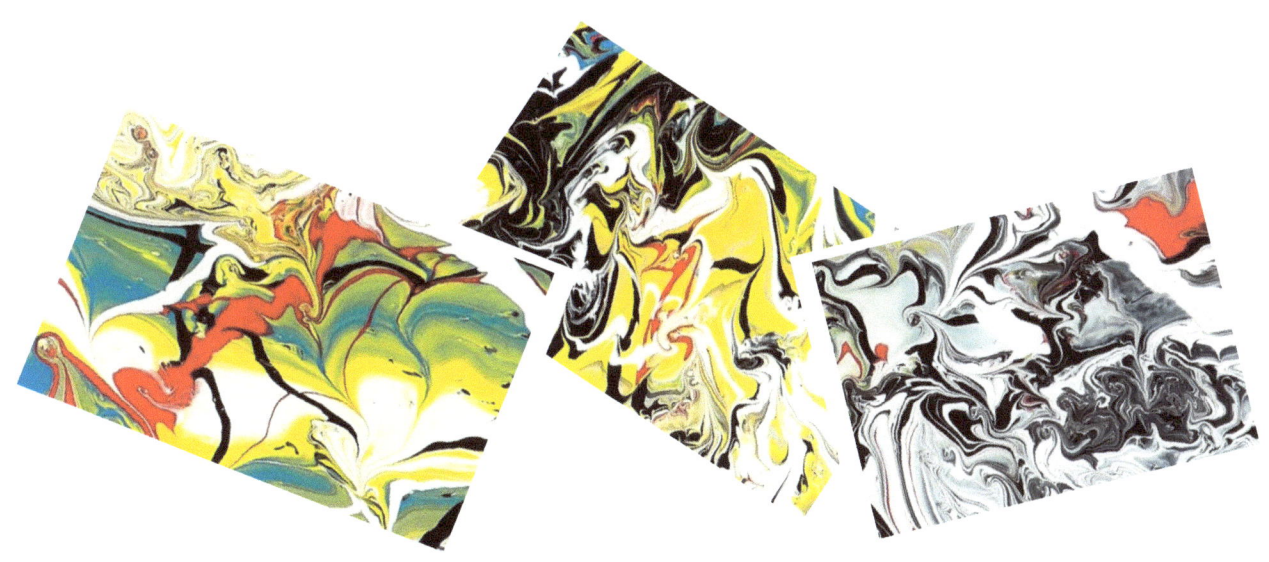

Do You Love Me?

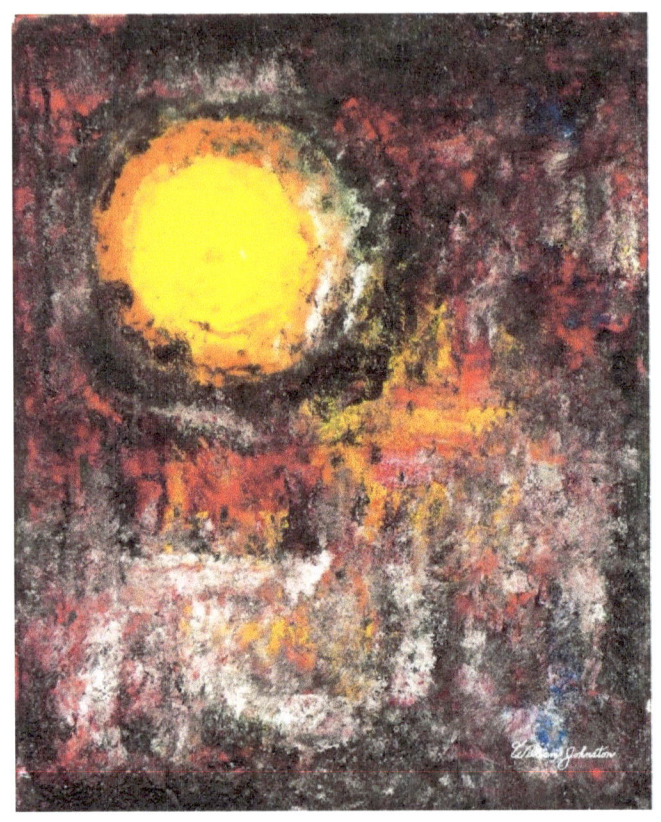

If you Love Me, You will keep my commandments.   *John 14:15*

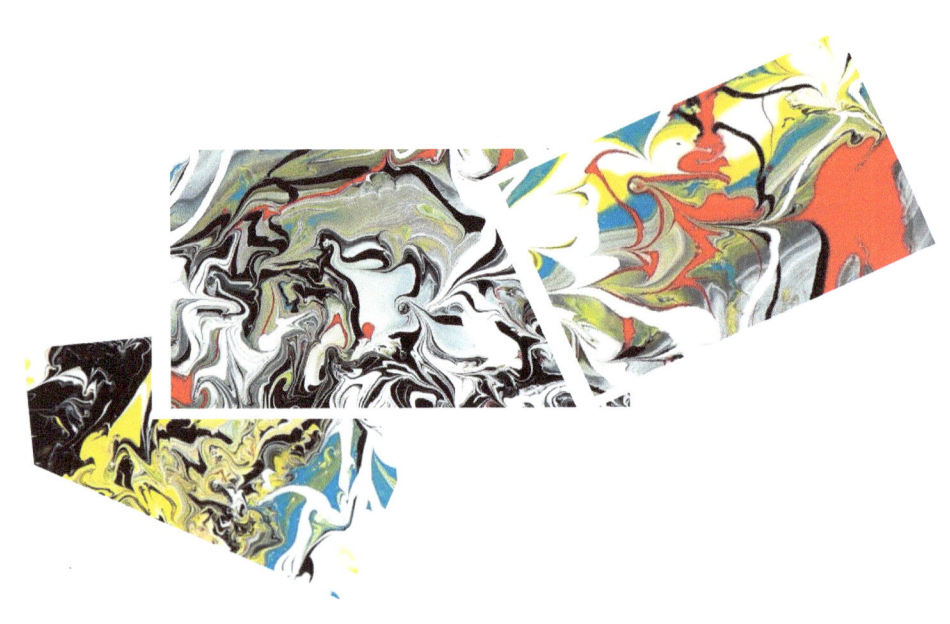

Love One Another

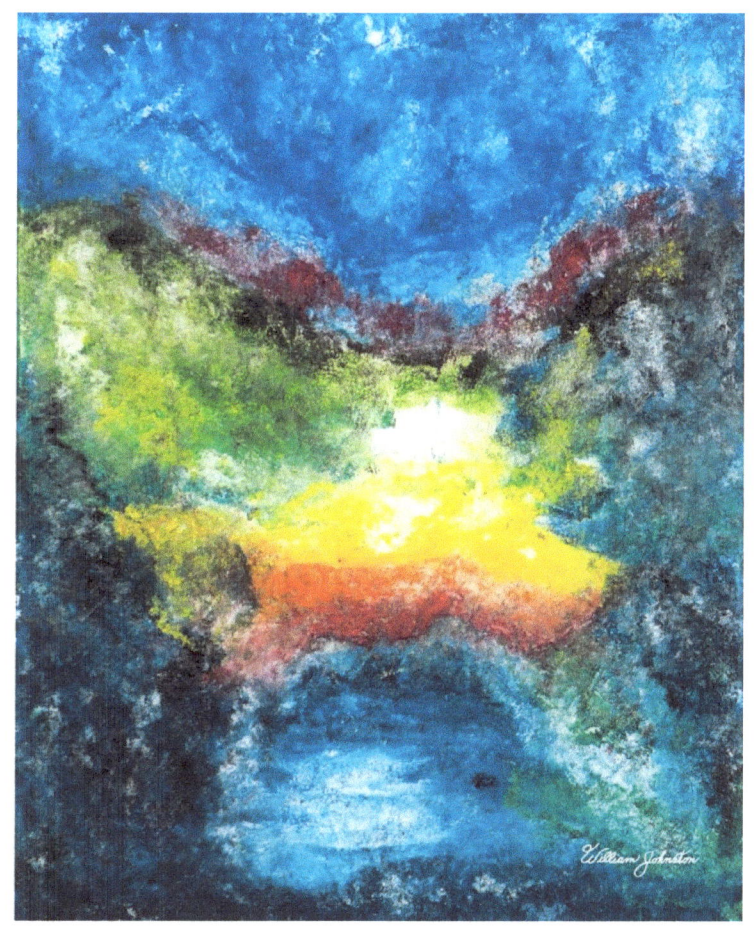

Love one another, just as I have loved you.

John 13:34

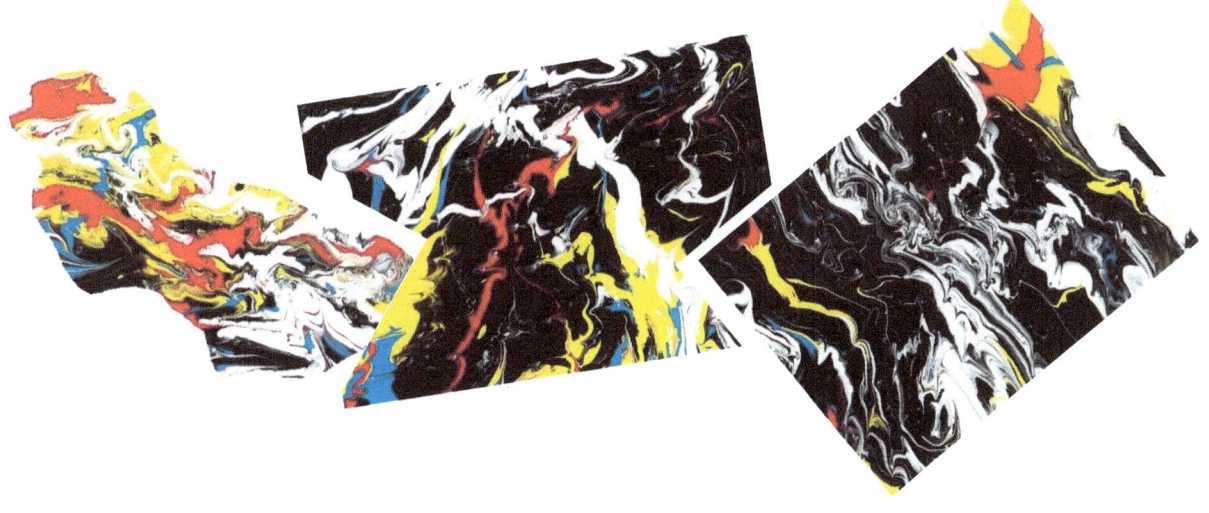

A Friend Loves

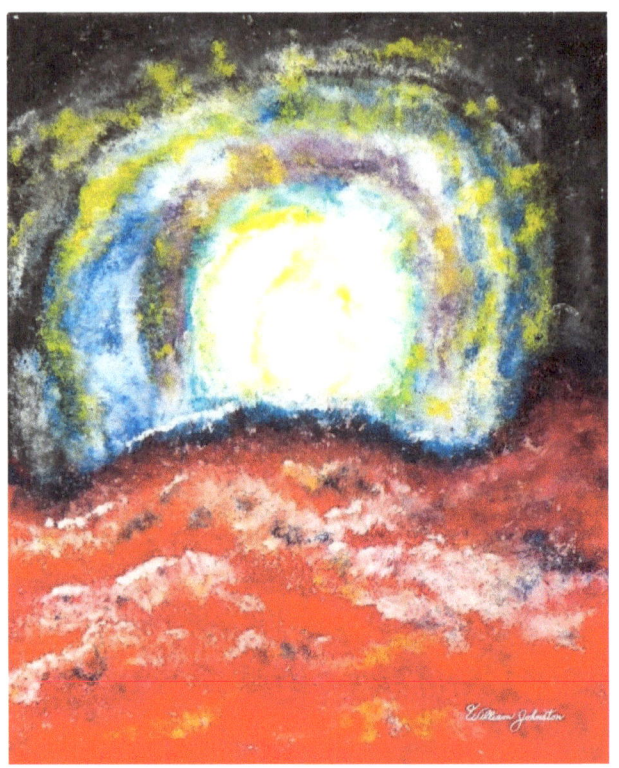

A Friend Loves at all times, and a brother is born for Adversity.

Proverbs 17:17

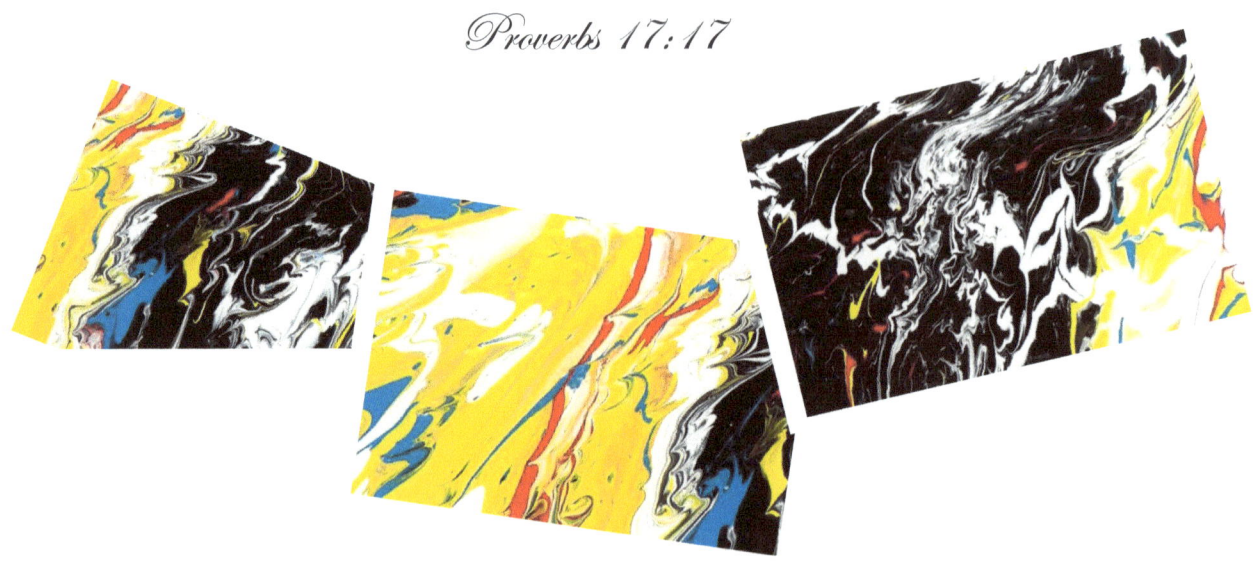

Love your Neighbor

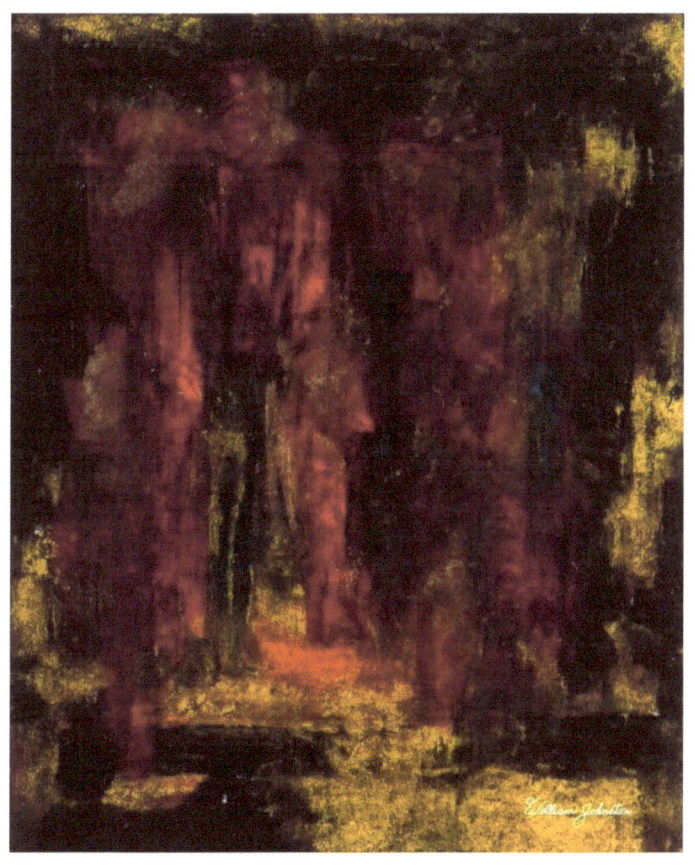

You shall love your neighbor as yourself.

Mark 12:31

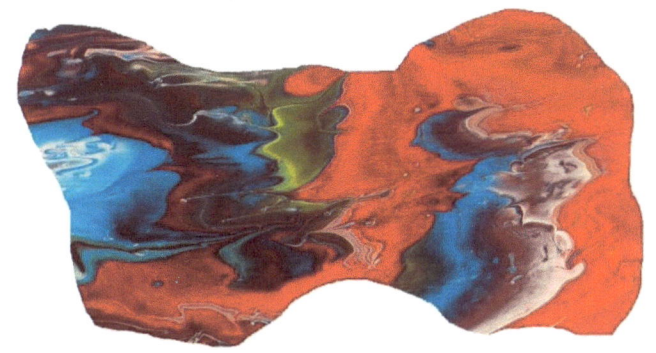

Love is from God

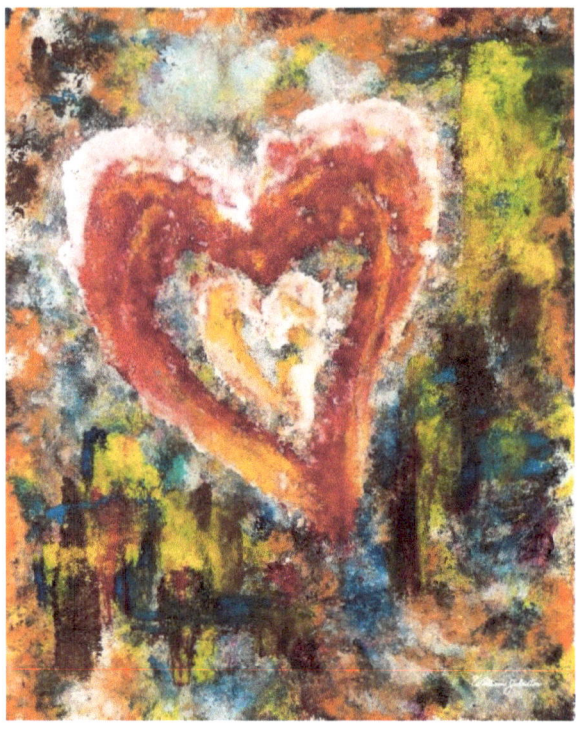

Let us love one another, for love is from God, and whoever loves has been born of God and knows God.   *1 John 4:7*

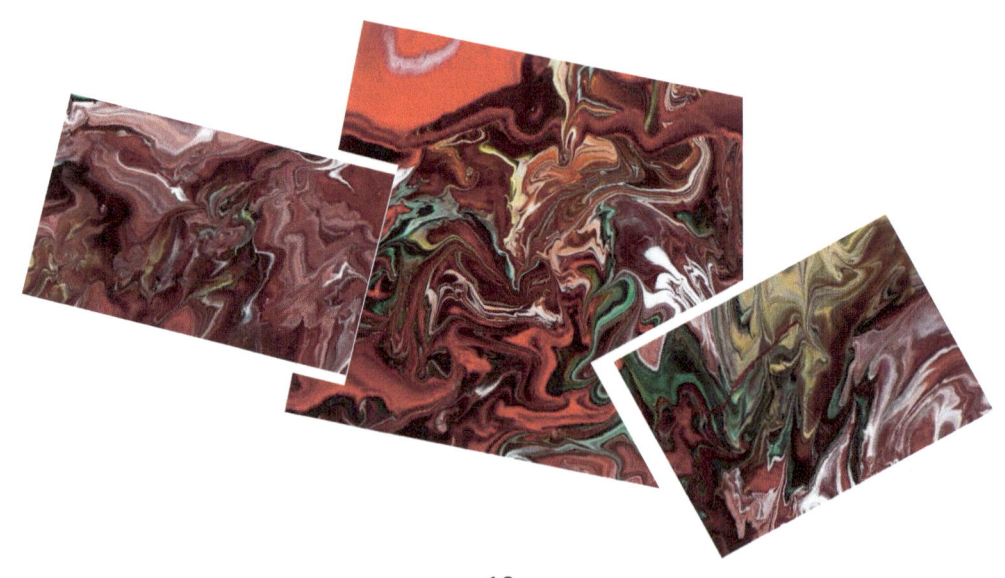

Love Your Enemies

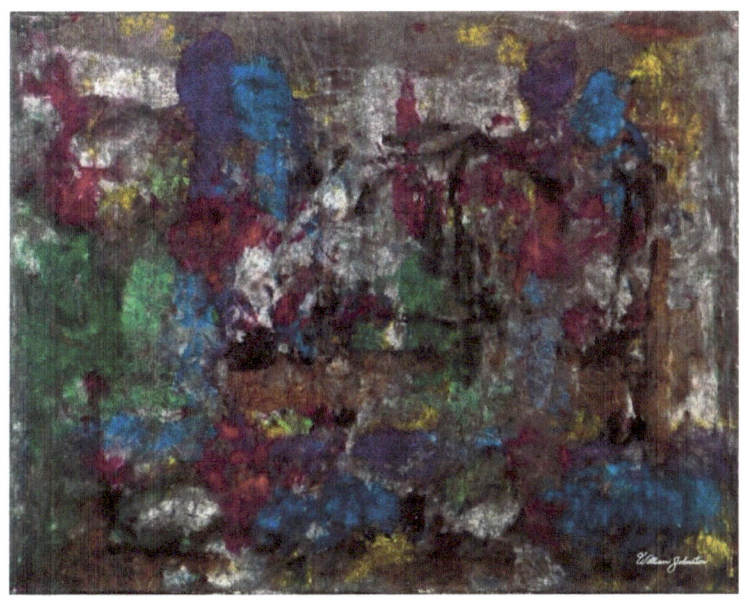

But love your enemies, do good to them and lend to them without expecting to get anything back.   *Luke 6:35*

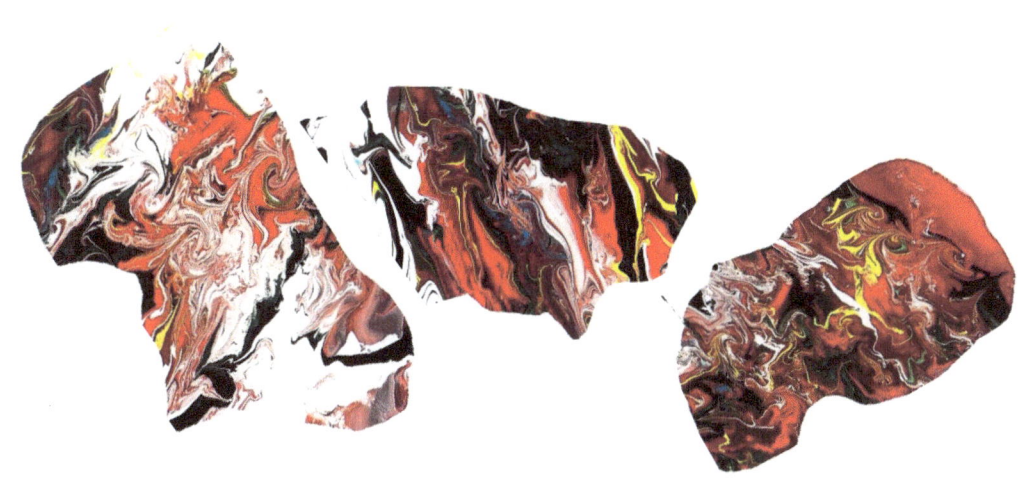

He First Loved Us

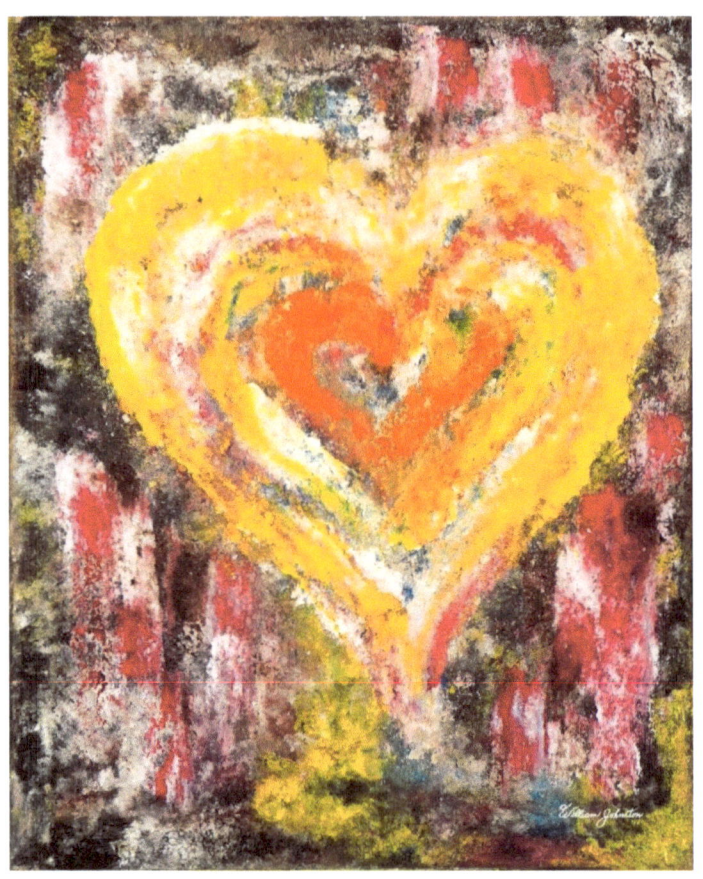

There is no fear in love. But perfect love drives out fear. because fear has to do with punishment. The one who fears is not made perfect in love. We love because He first loved us.   1 John 4:18-19

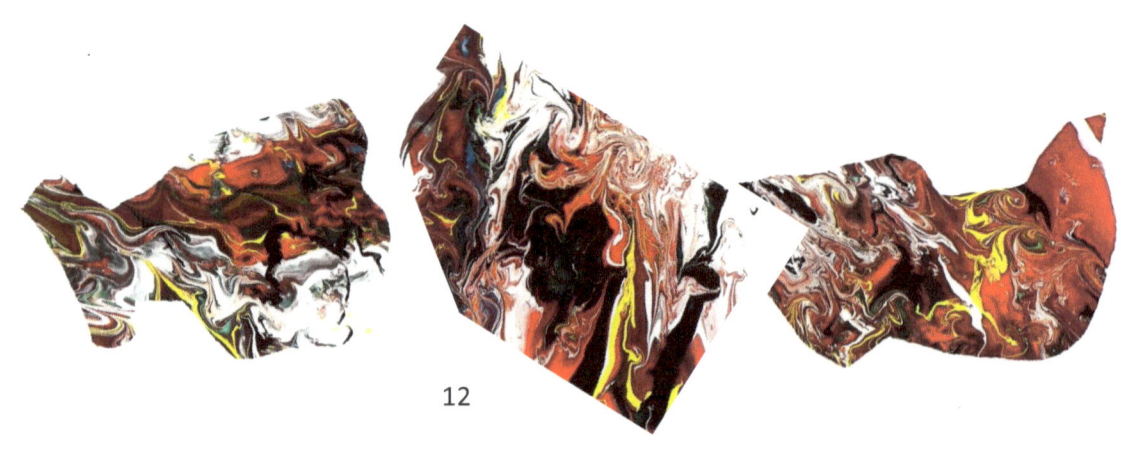

Perfect Love

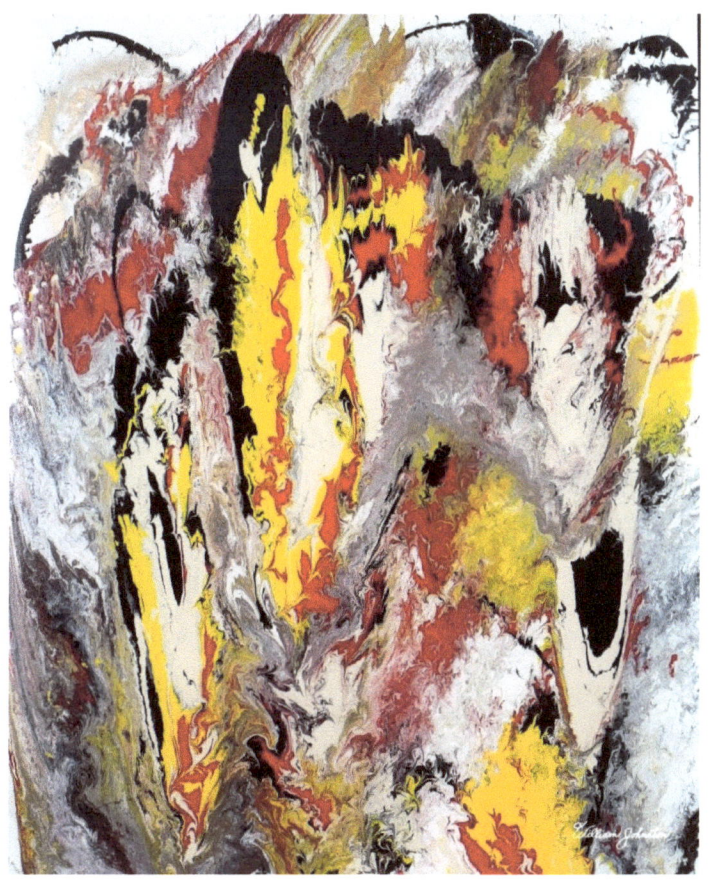

And over all these virtues put on Love, which binds them all together in perfect unity.

Colossians 3:14

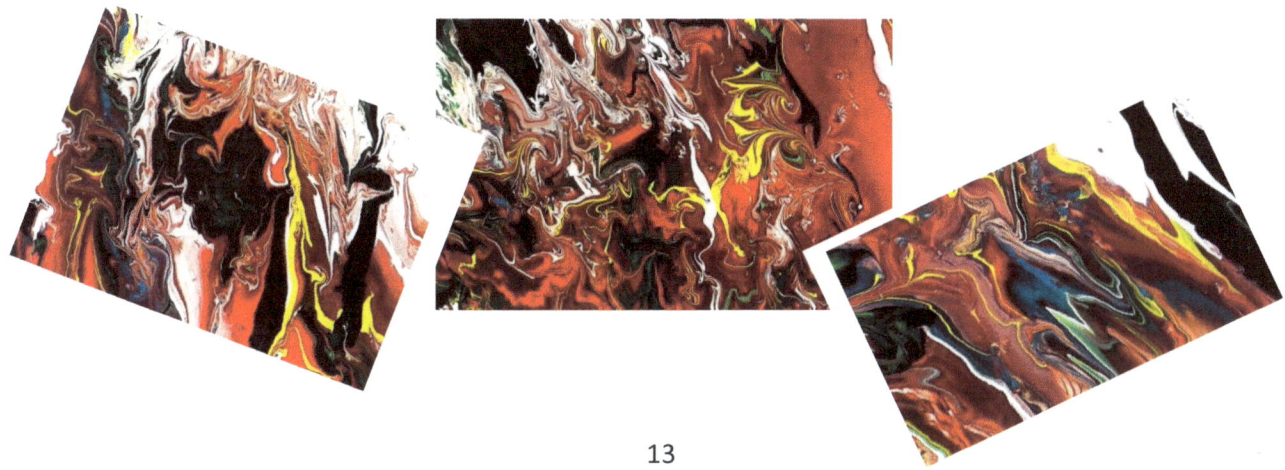

Eternal Life

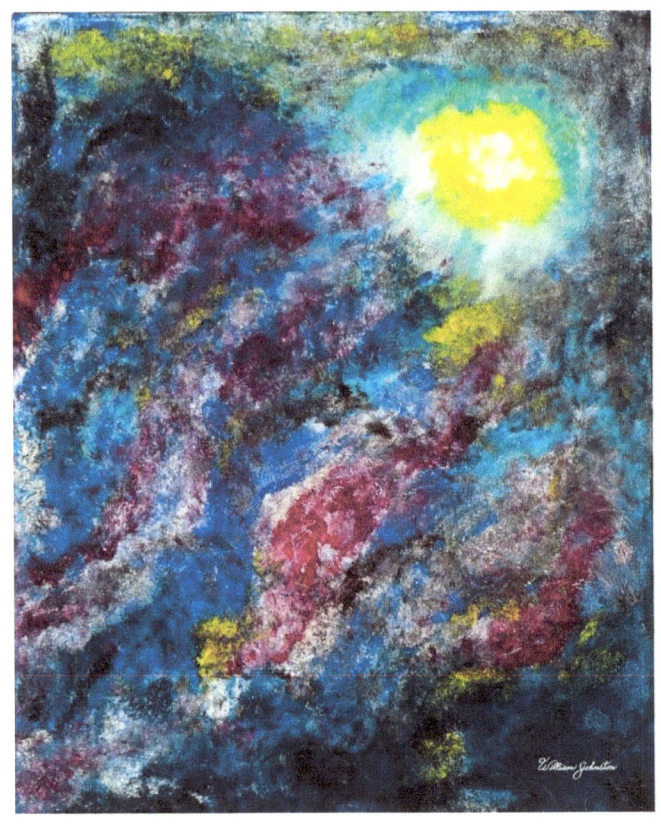

For God so loved the world that He gave His only Son that whoever believes in Him should not perish but have eternal life. John 3:16

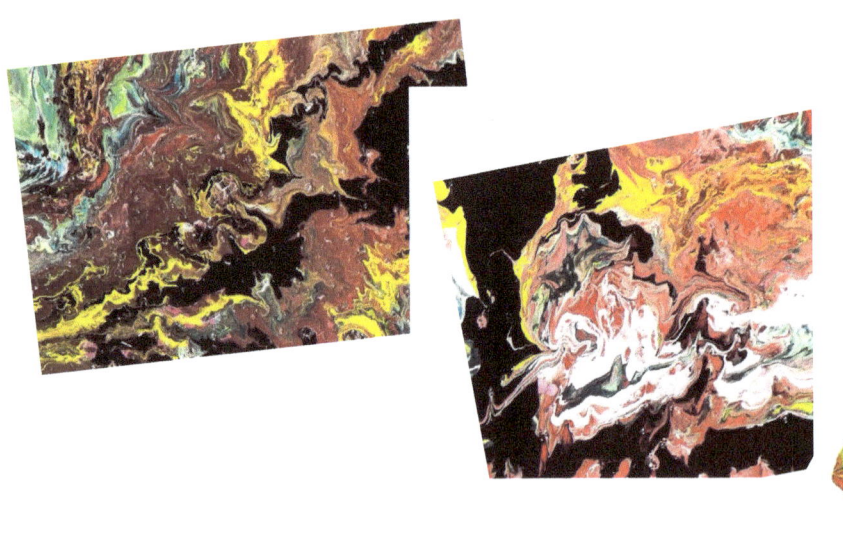

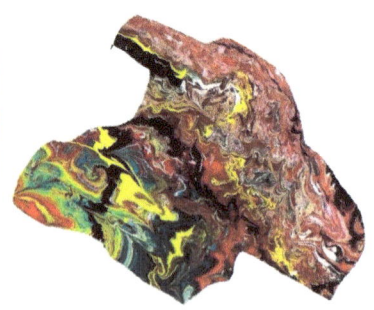

Holy Dwelling

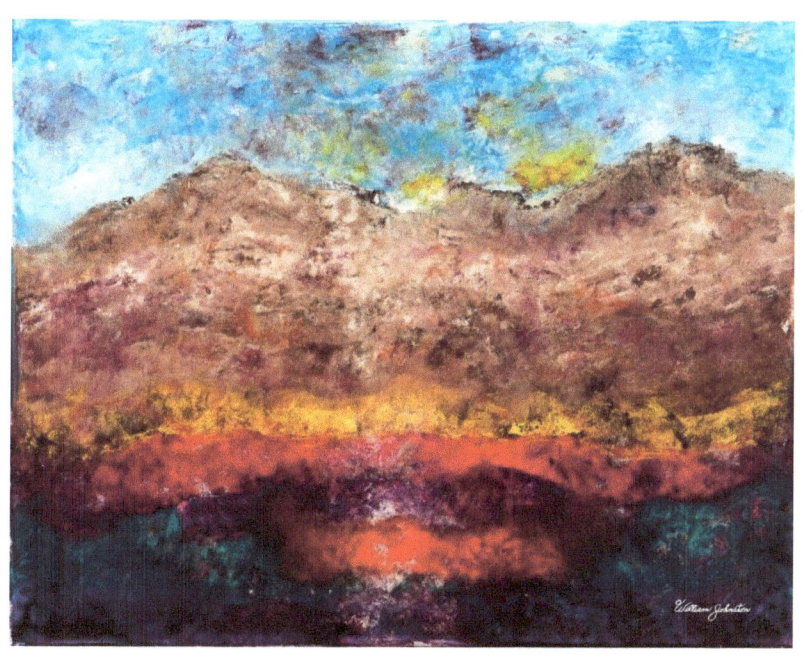

In your unfailing love you will lead the people you have redeemed. In your strength you will guide them to your holy dwelling.   *Exodus 15:13*

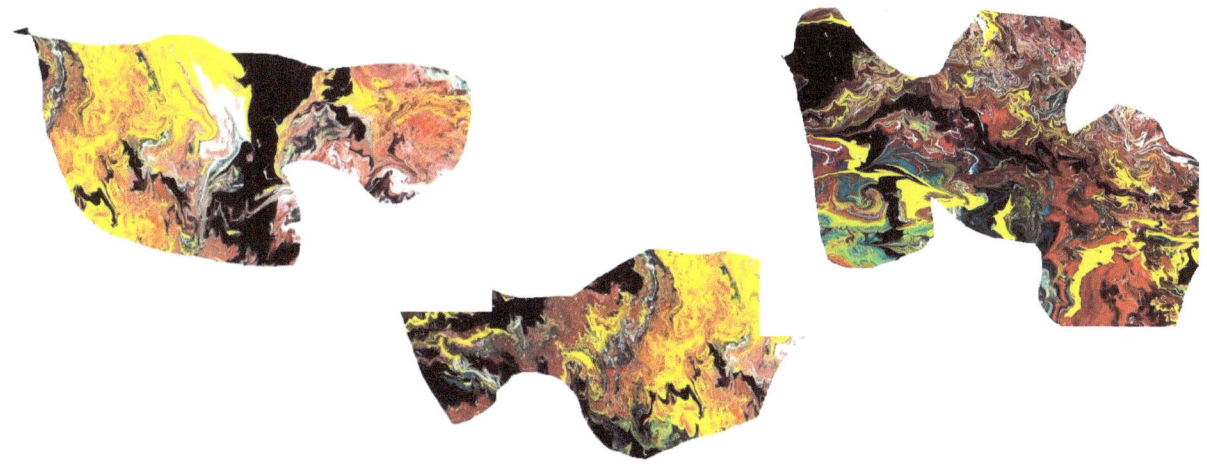

Love your Neighbor

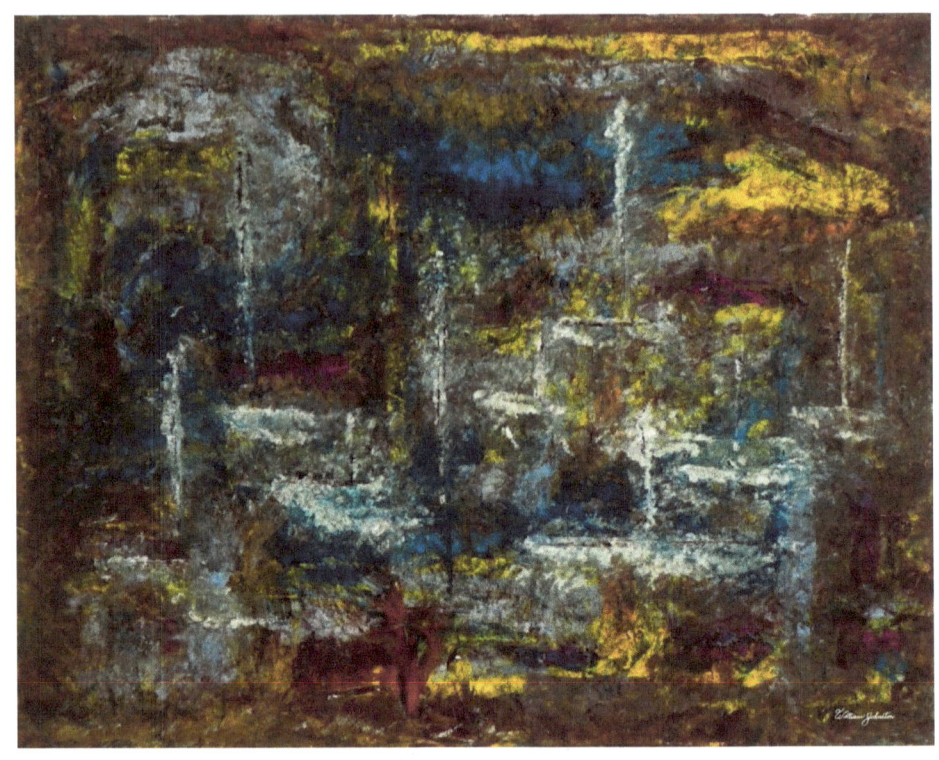

Do not seek revenge or bear a grudge against one of your people, but love your neighbor as yourself. I am the LORD. Leviticus 19:18

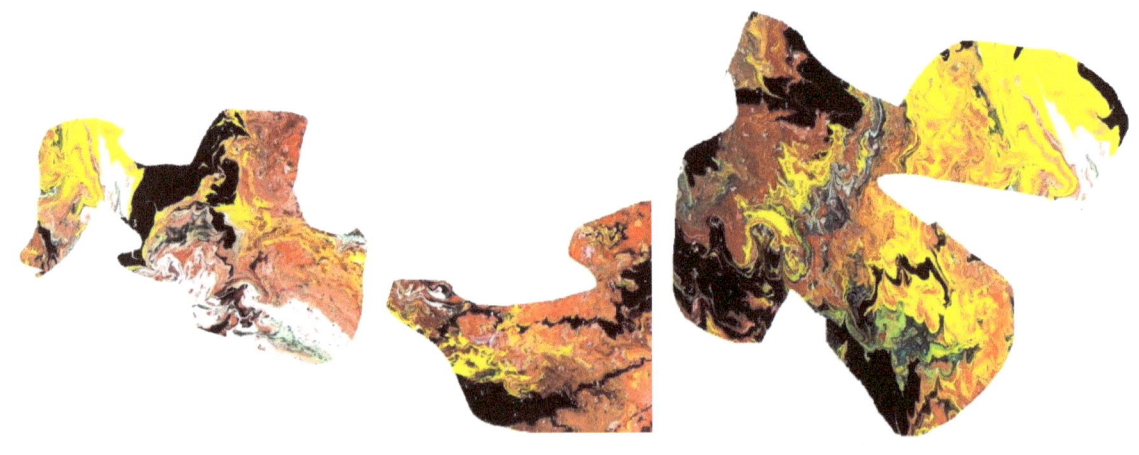

The Lord Is One

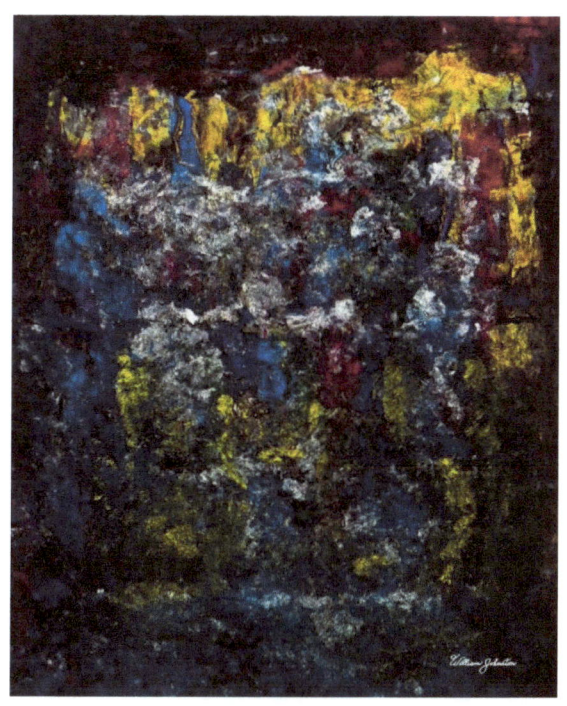

Hear, O Israel: The LORD our God, the LORD is one. Love the LORD your God with all your heart and with all your soul and with all your strength. These commandments that I give you today are to be upon your hearts. Deuteronomy 6:4-6

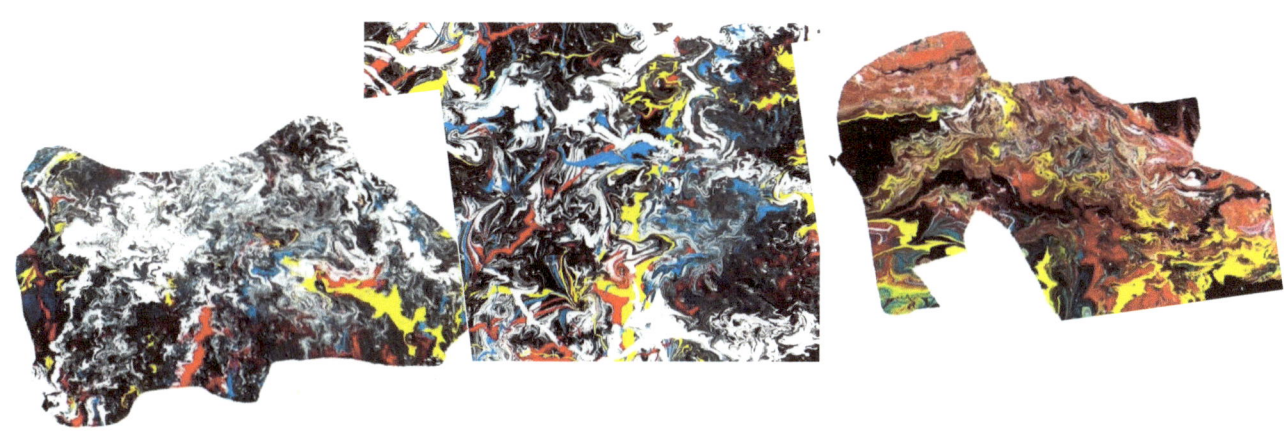

The Law Of Moses

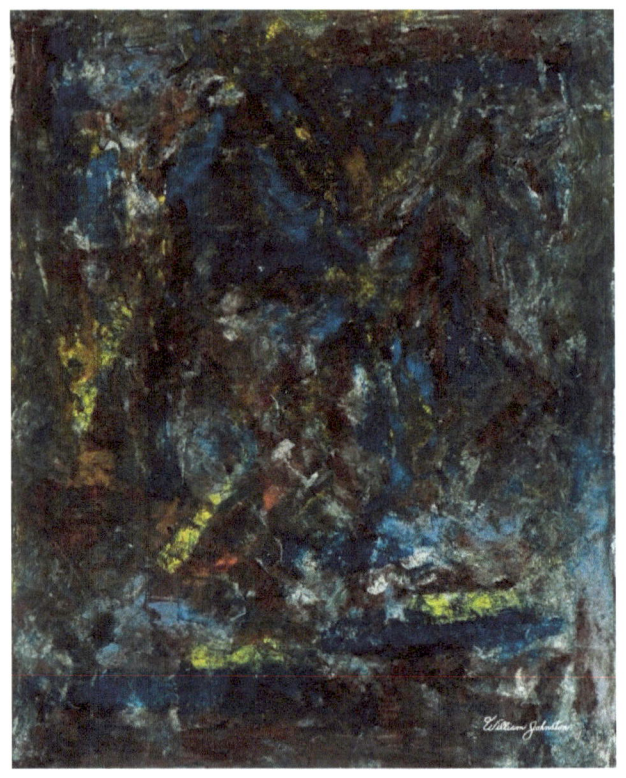

But be very careful to keep the commandment and the law that Moses the servant of the LORD gave you: to love the LORD your God, to walk in all his ways, to obey his commands, to hold fast to him and to serve him with all your heart and all your soul.

Joshua 22:5

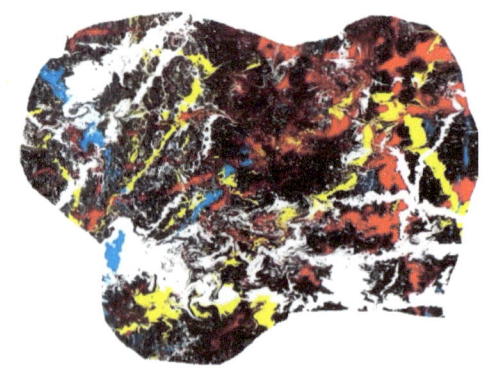

Give Thanks

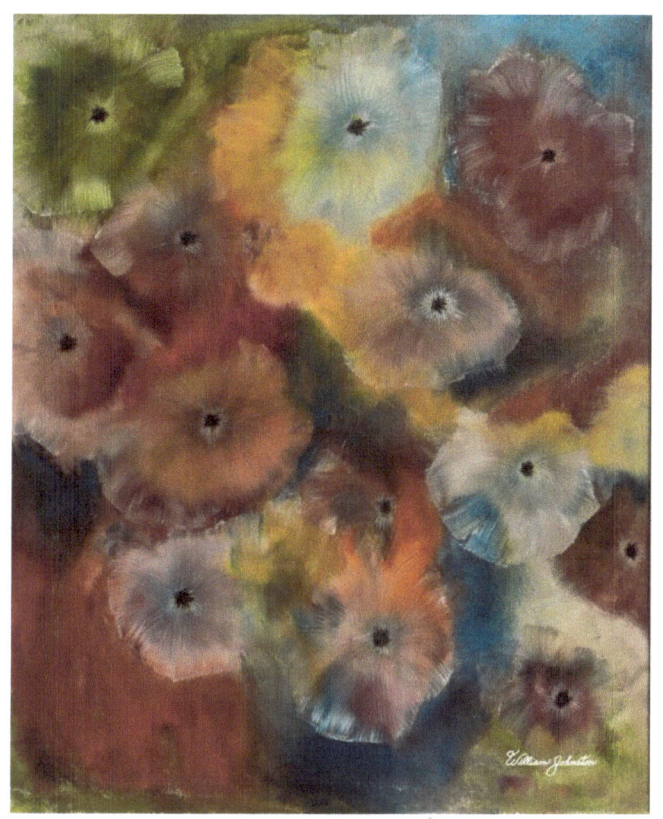

Give thanks to the LORD, for he is good; his love endures forever.

1 Chronicles 16:34

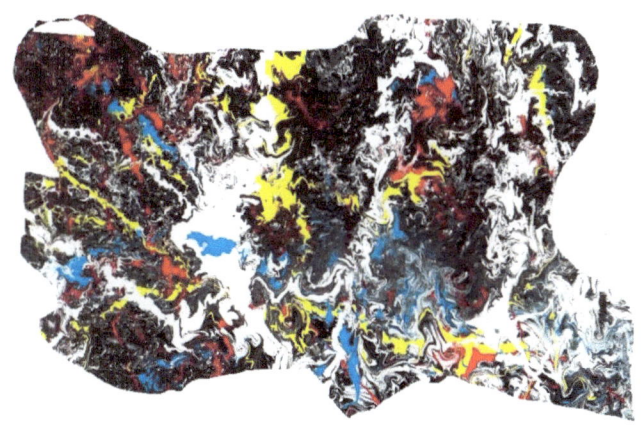

Rejoice

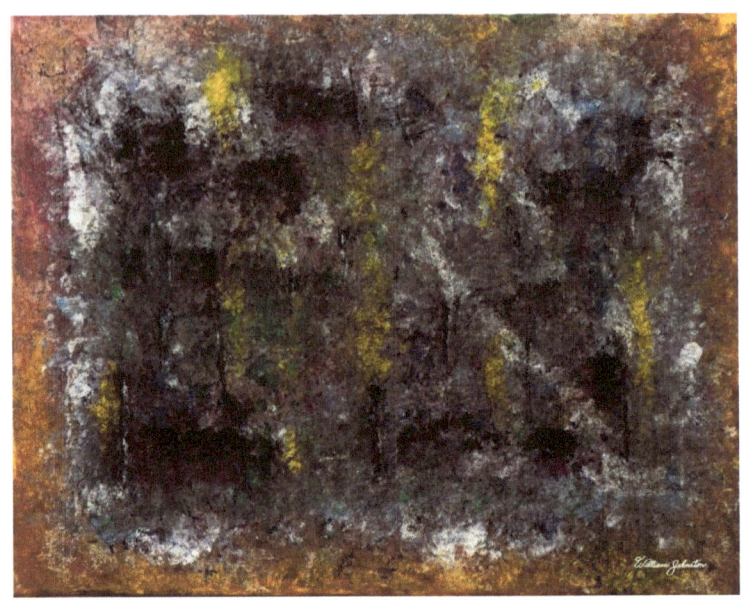

But let all who take refuge in you be glad; let them ever sing for joy. Spread your protection over them that those who love your name may rejoice in you.

Psalm 5:11

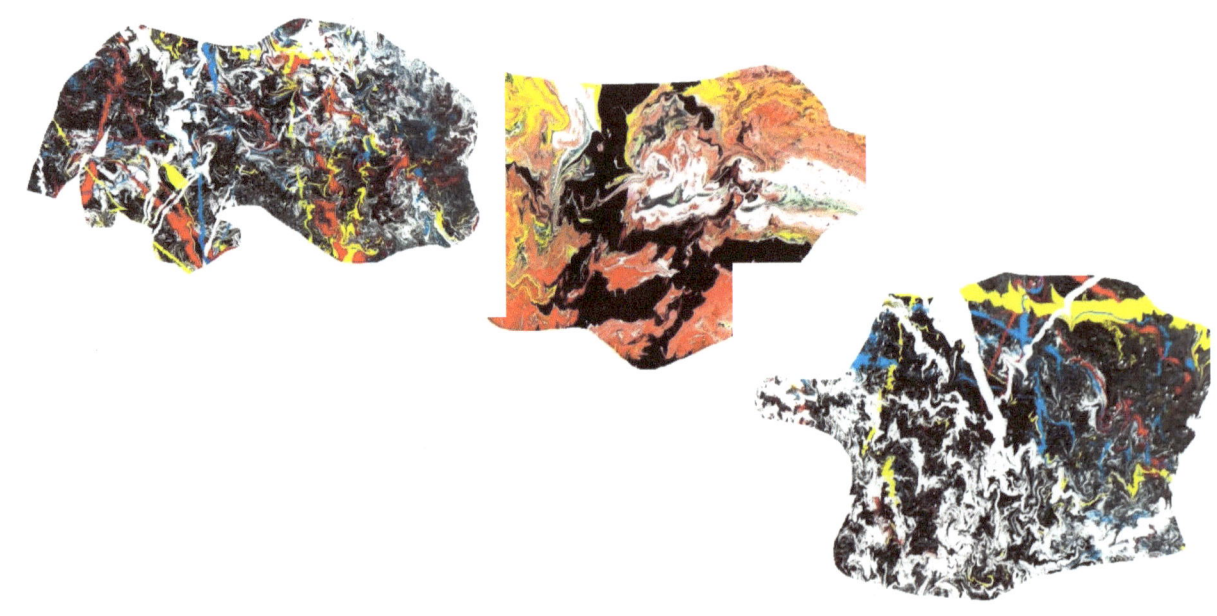

Unfailing Love

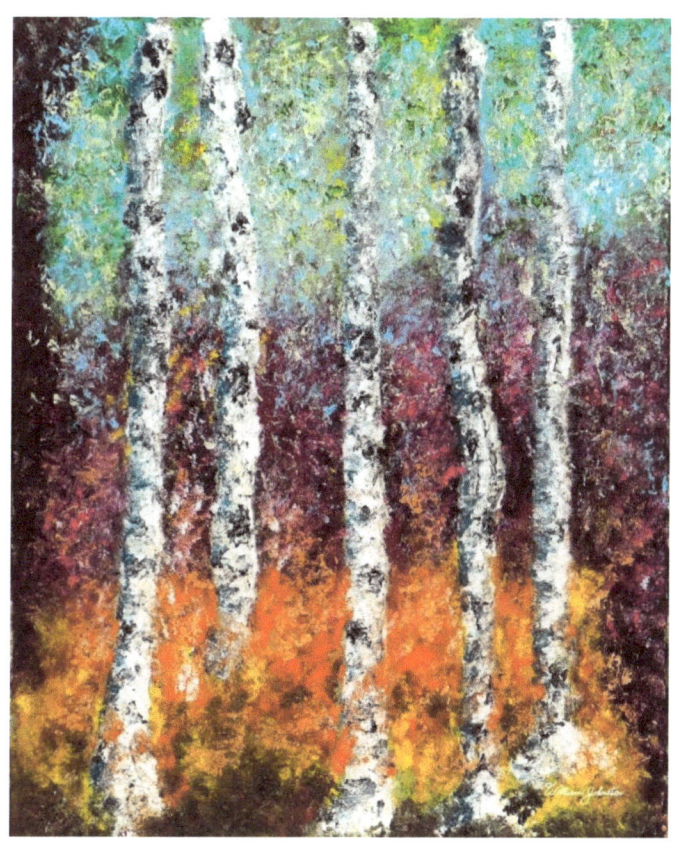

But I trust in your unfailing love; my heart rejoices in your salvation.

Psalm 13:5

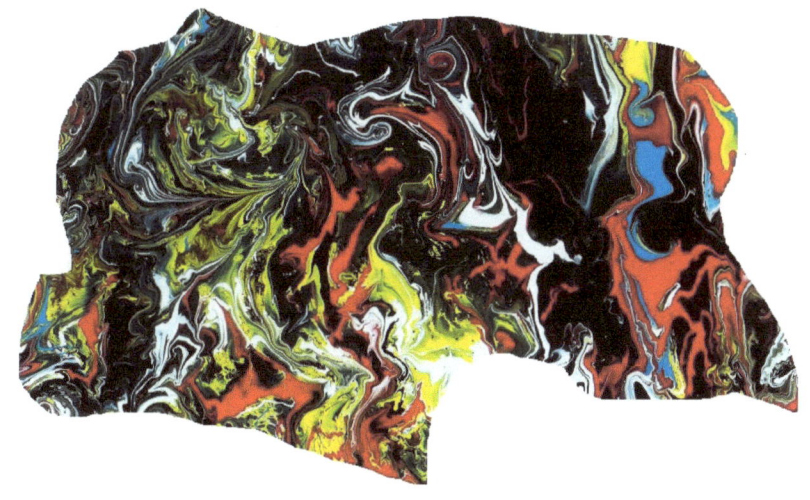

Loving

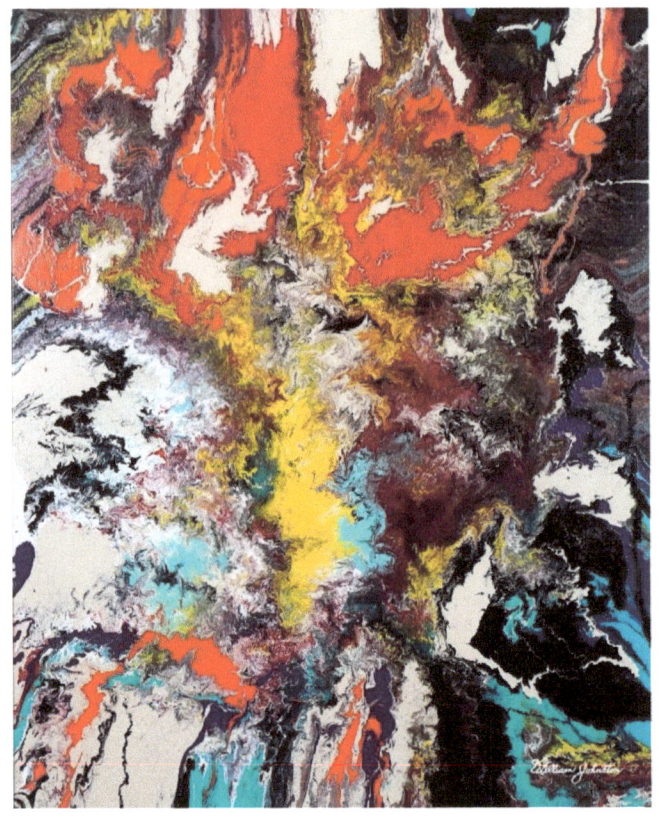

You prepare a table before me in the presence of my enemies. You anoint my head with oil; my cup overflows. Surely goodness and love will follow me all the days of my life, and I will dwell in the house of the LORD forever.   Psalm 23:5-6

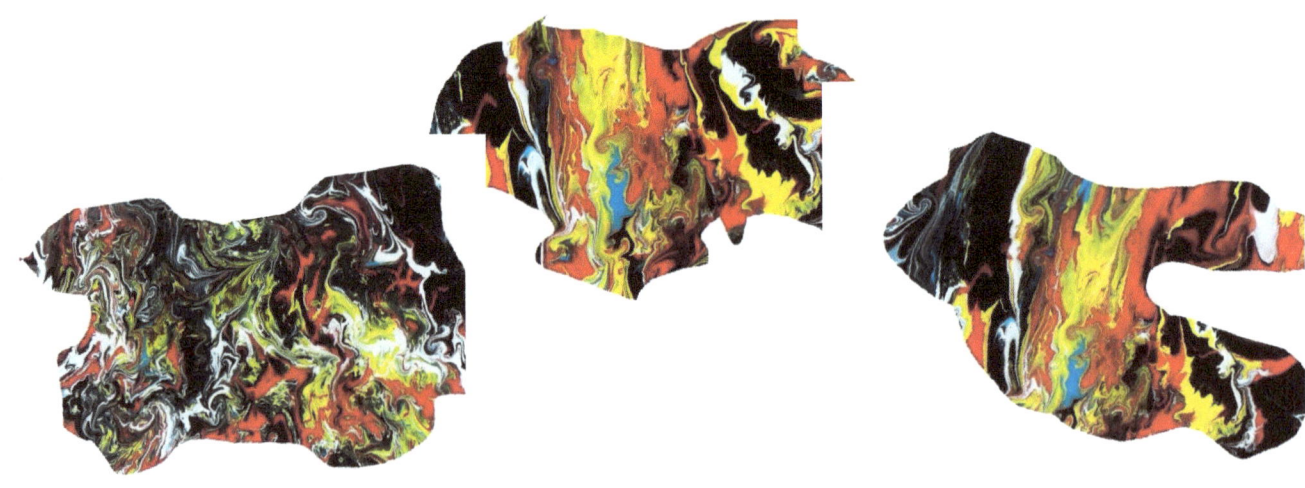

My Affliction

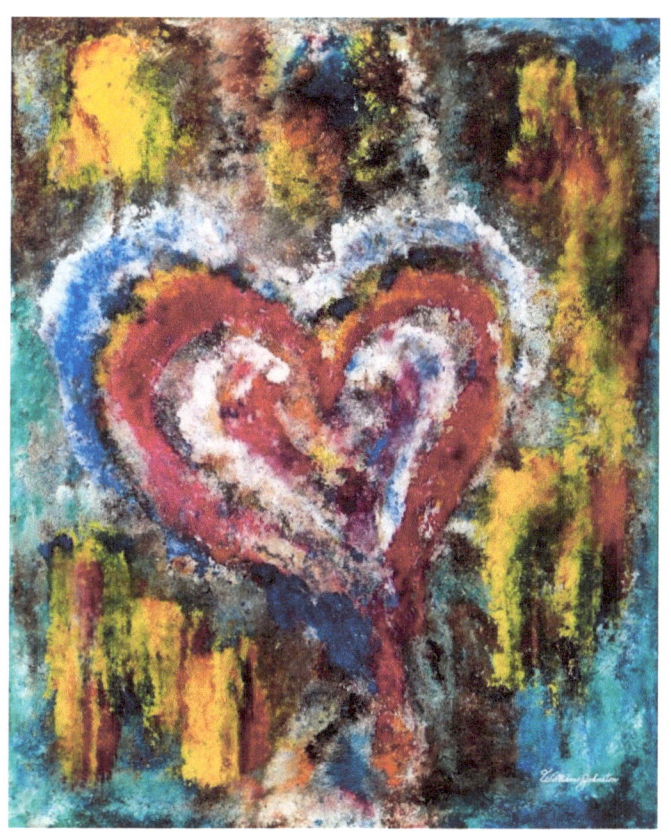

I will be glad and rejoice in your love, for you saw my affliction and knew the anguish of my soul. Psalm 31:7

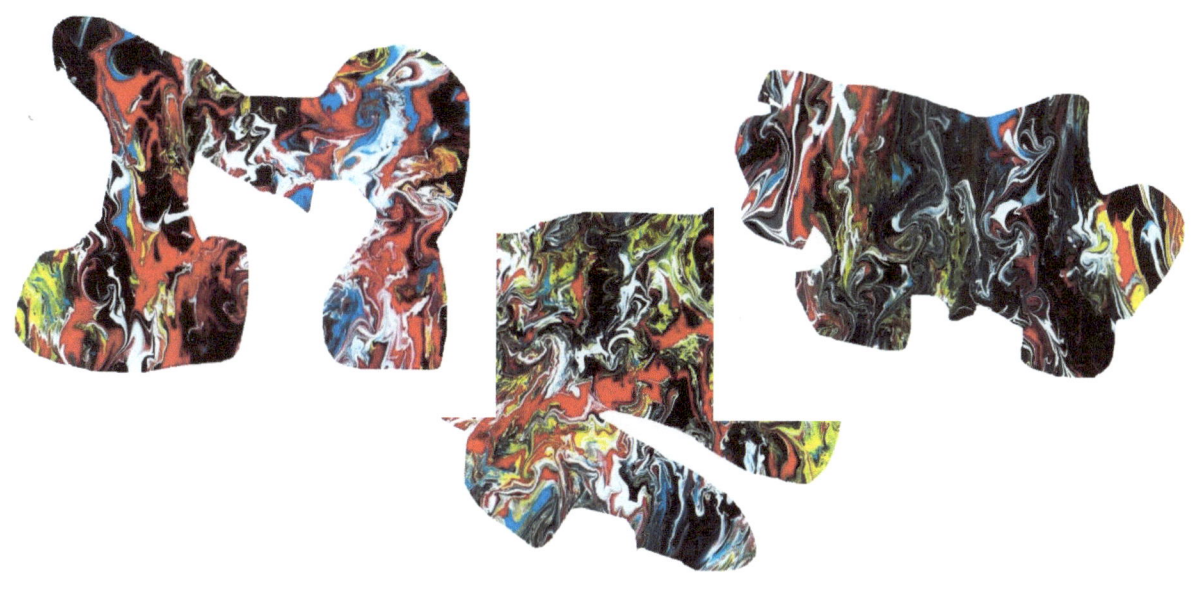

Love That Never Fails

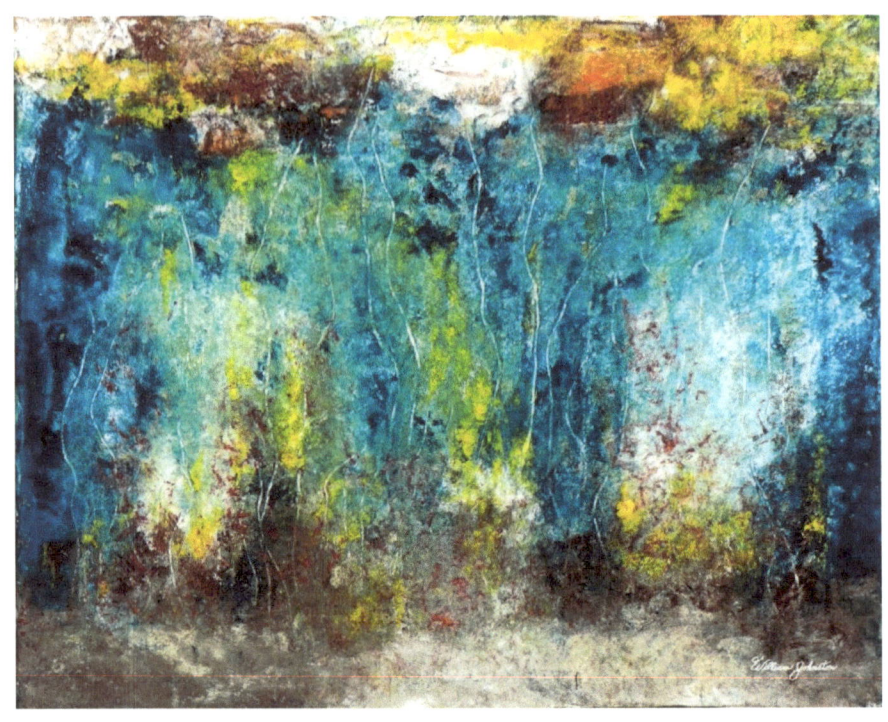

The LORD loves righteousness and justice; the earth is full of his unfailing love.

Psalm 33:5

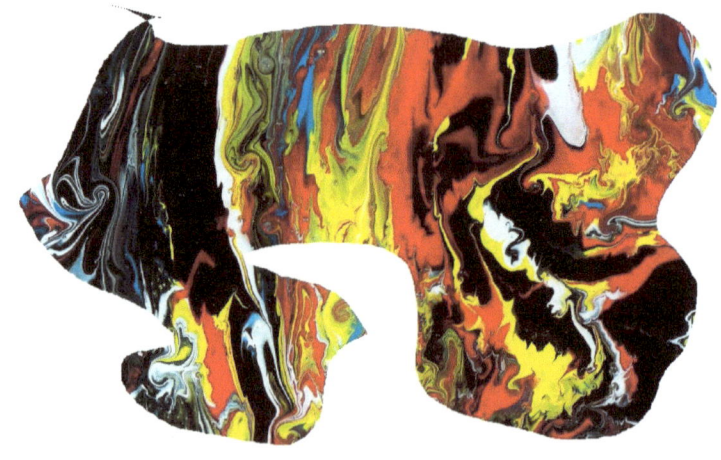

Your Love

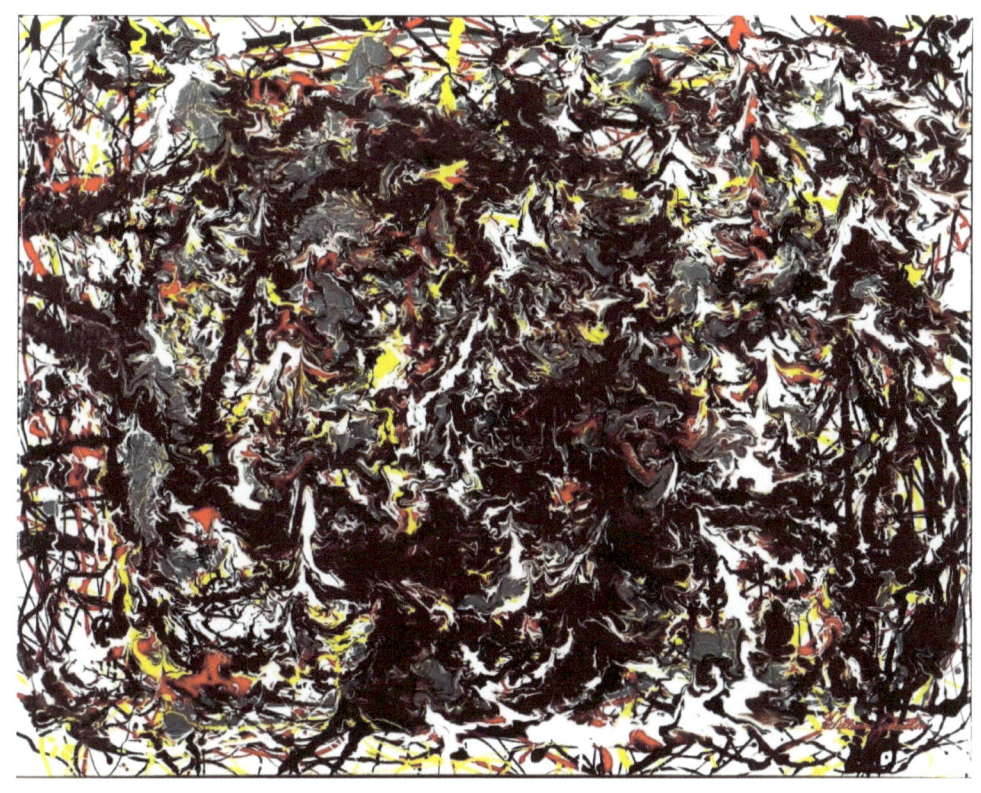

Your love, O LORD, reaches to the heavens, your faithfulness to the skies. Your righteousness is like the mighty mountains, your justice like the great deep. O LORD, you preserve both man and beast.   *Psalm 36:5-6*

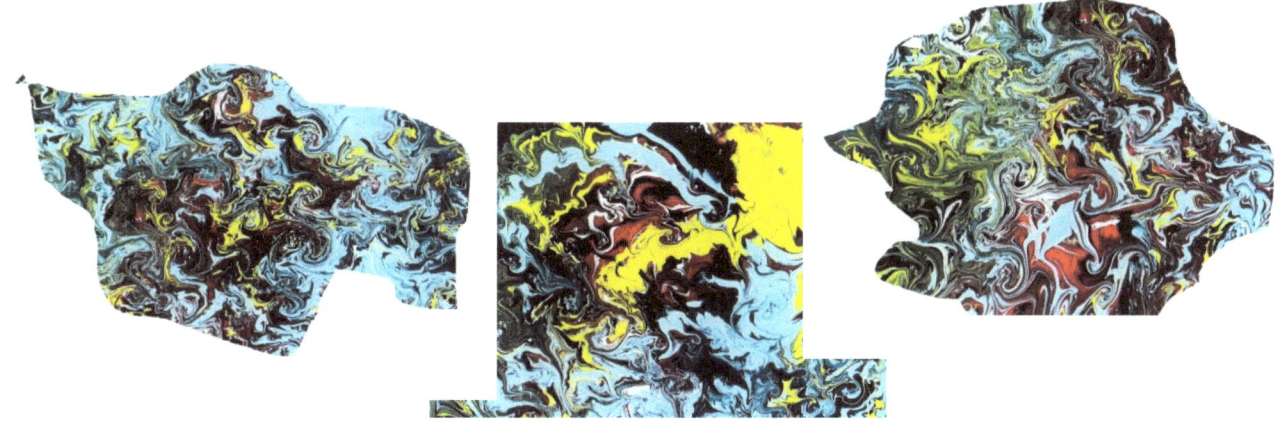

Mercy

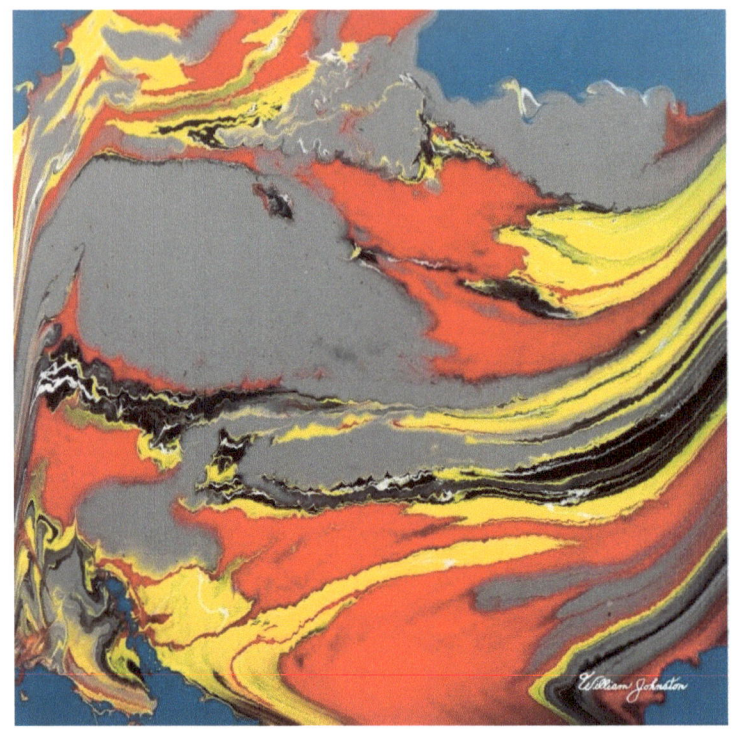

Do not withhold your mercy from me, O LORD. Psalm 40:11

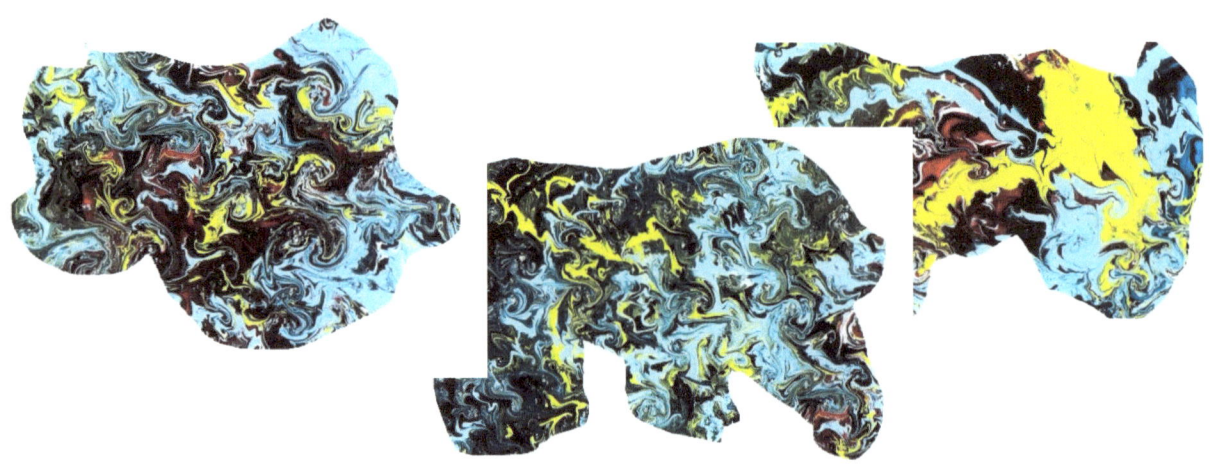

My Fortress

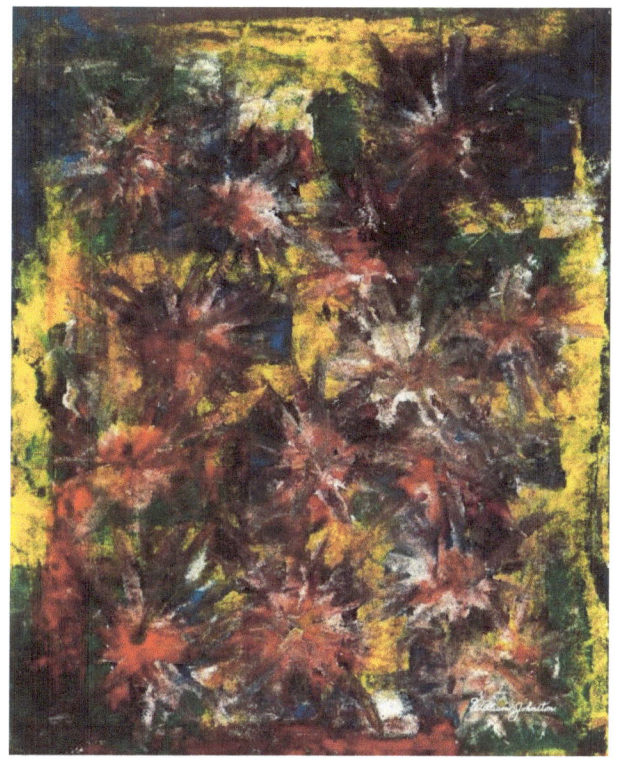

But I will sing of your strength, in the morning I will sing of your love; for you are my fortress, my refuge in times of trouble.

Psalm 59:16

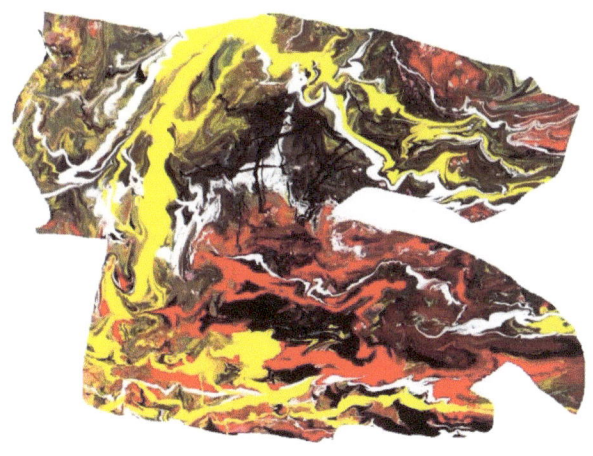

Love and Faithfulness

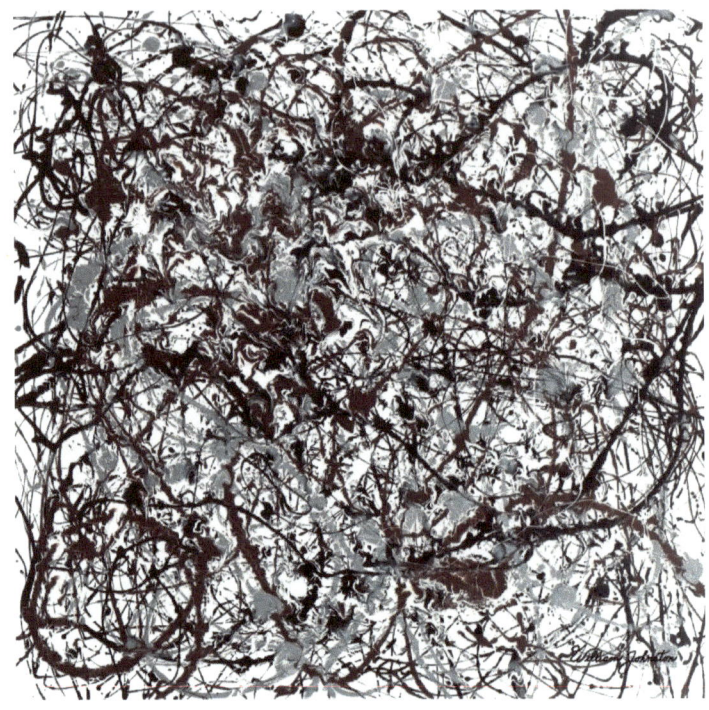

Love and faithfulness meet together; righteousness and peace kiss each other.

Psalm 85:10

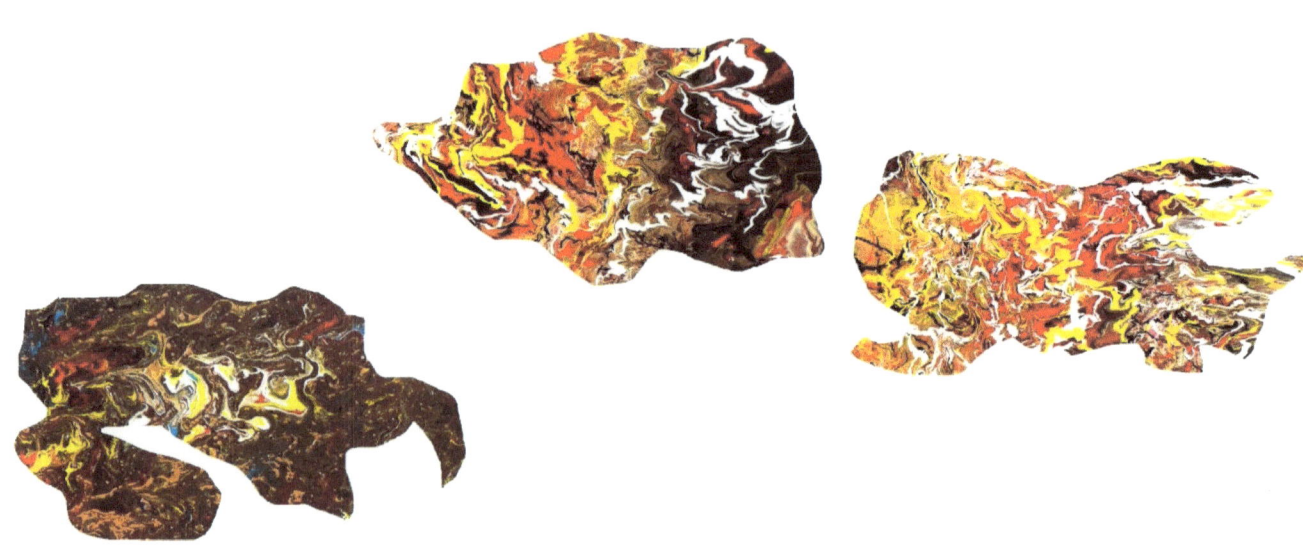

You are Forgiving and Good

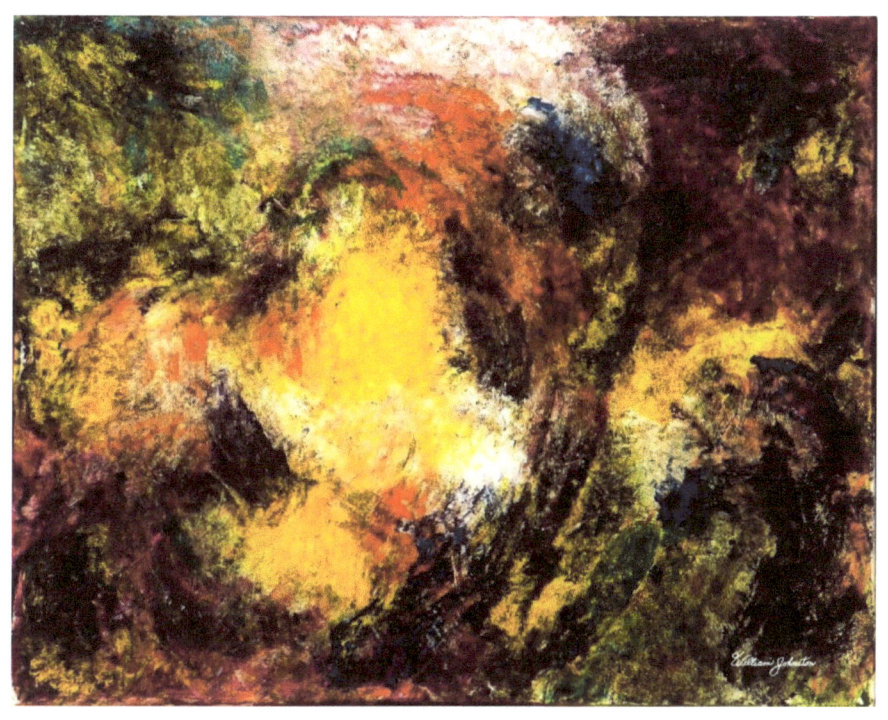

You are forgiving and good, O Lord, abounding in love to all who call to you.

Psalm 86:5

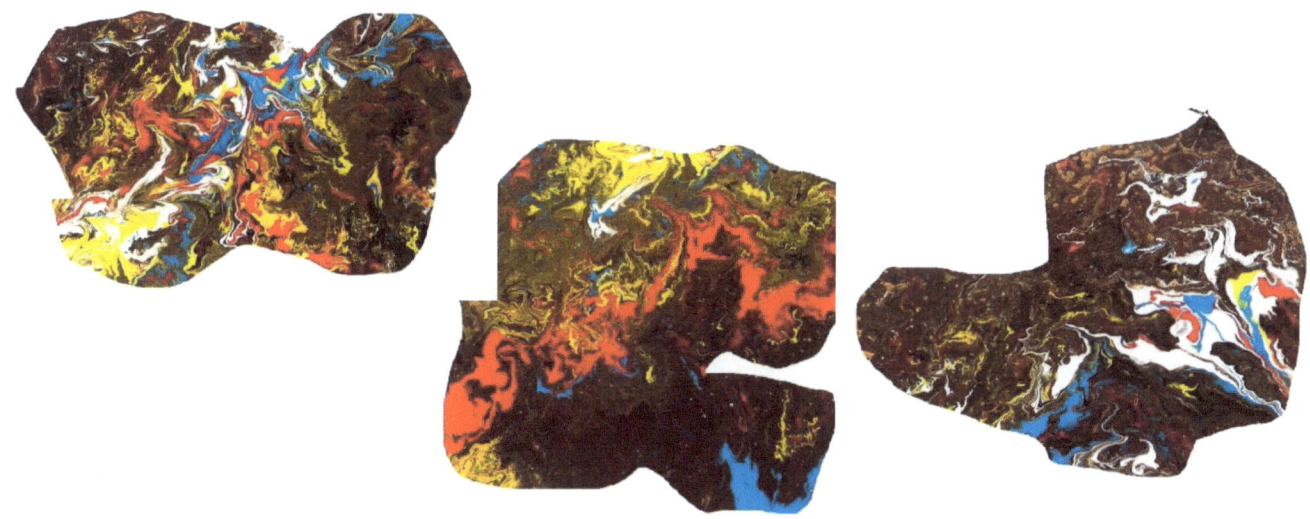

The Tablet Of Your Heart

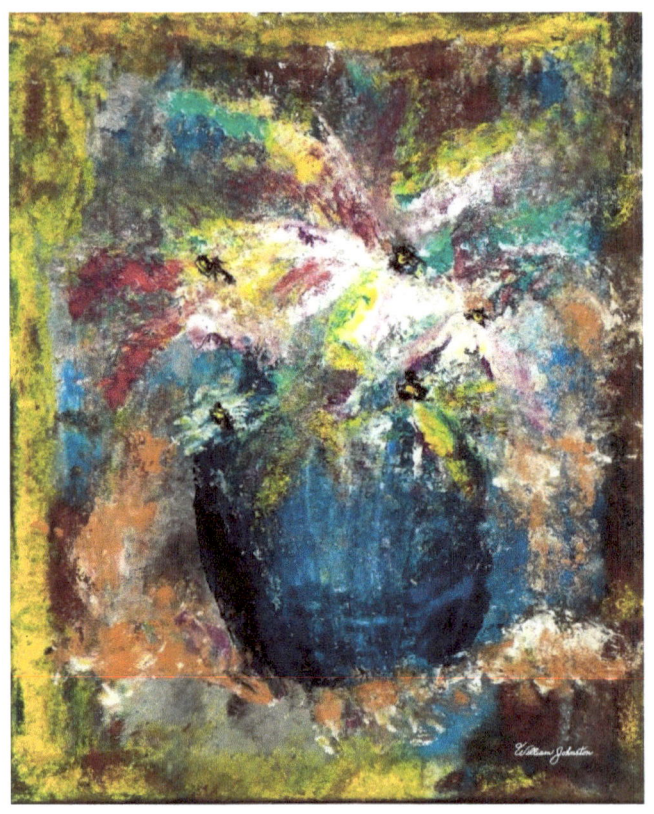

Let love and faithfulness never leave you; bind them around your neck, write them on the tablet of your heart.

Proverbs 3:3

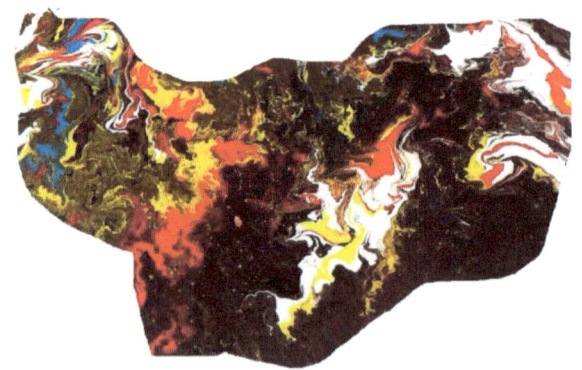

The Light of Christ

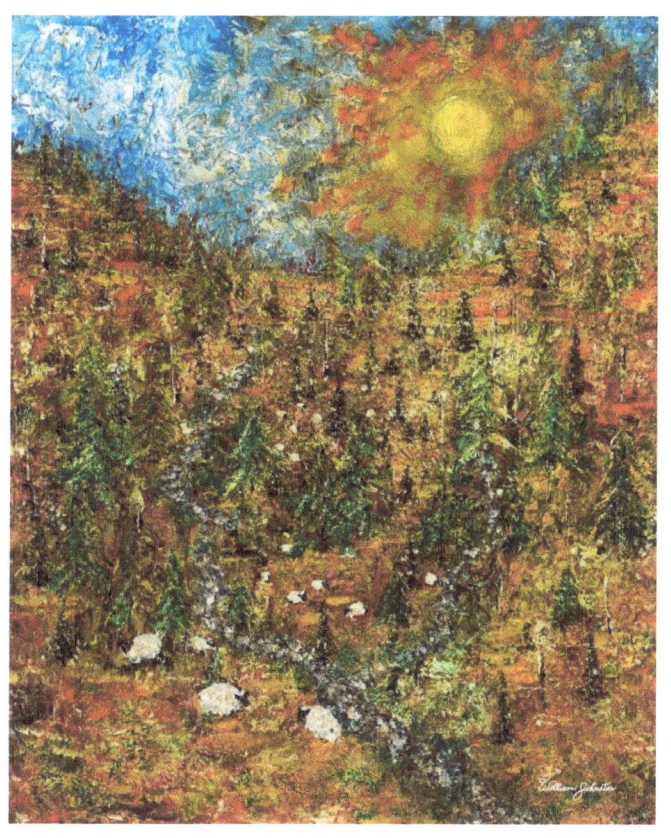

Jesus said, "I am the light of the world. Whoever follows me will never walk in darkness, but will have the light of life." John 8:12

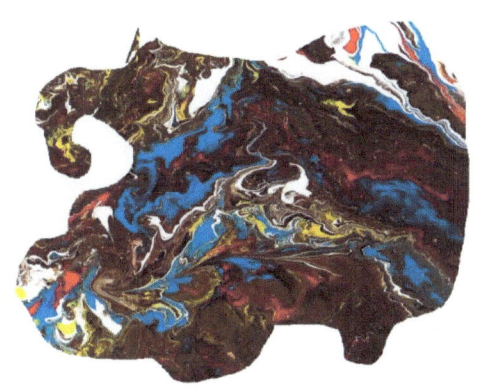

Prosperity and Honor

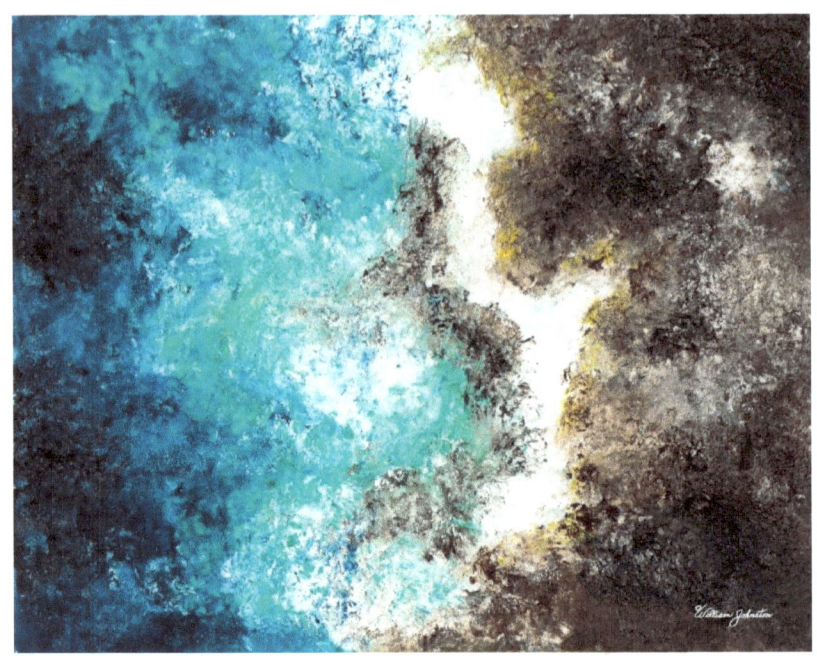

He who pursues righteousness and love finds life, prosperity and honor.

Proverbs 21:21

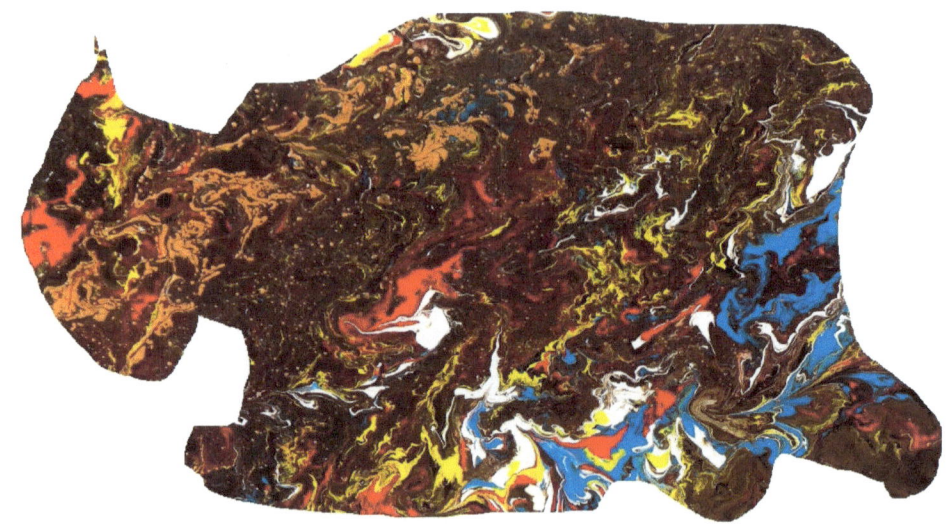

Covenant of Peace

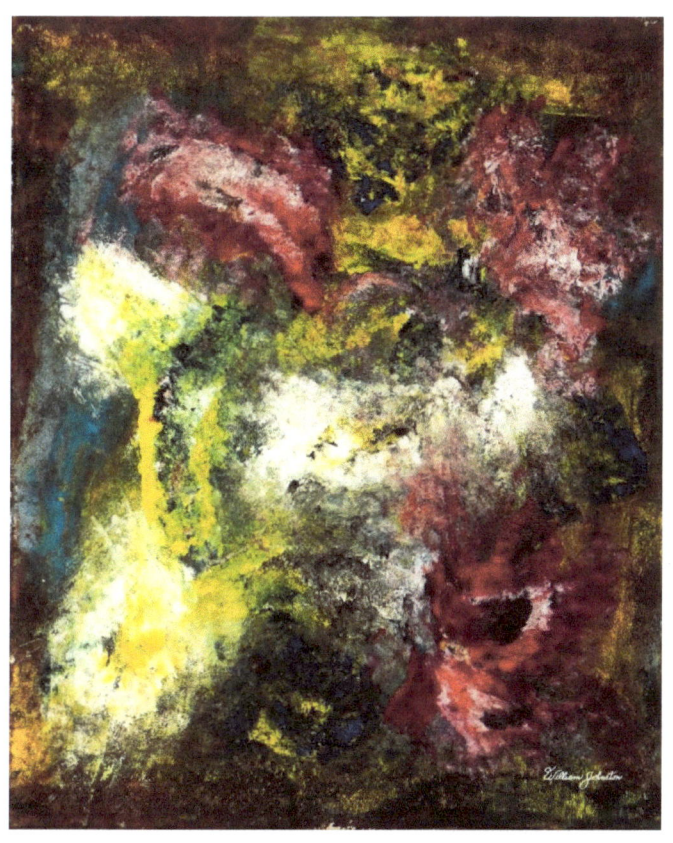

Though the mountains be shaken and the hills be removed, yet my unfailing love for you will not be shaken nor my covenant of peace be removed, says the LORD, who has compassion on you.   Isaiah 54:10

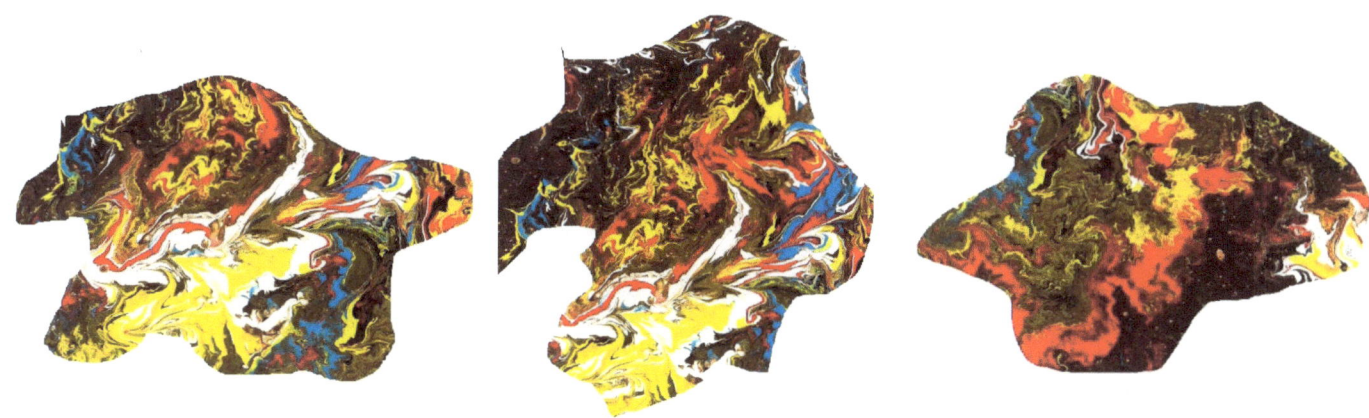

His Compassions

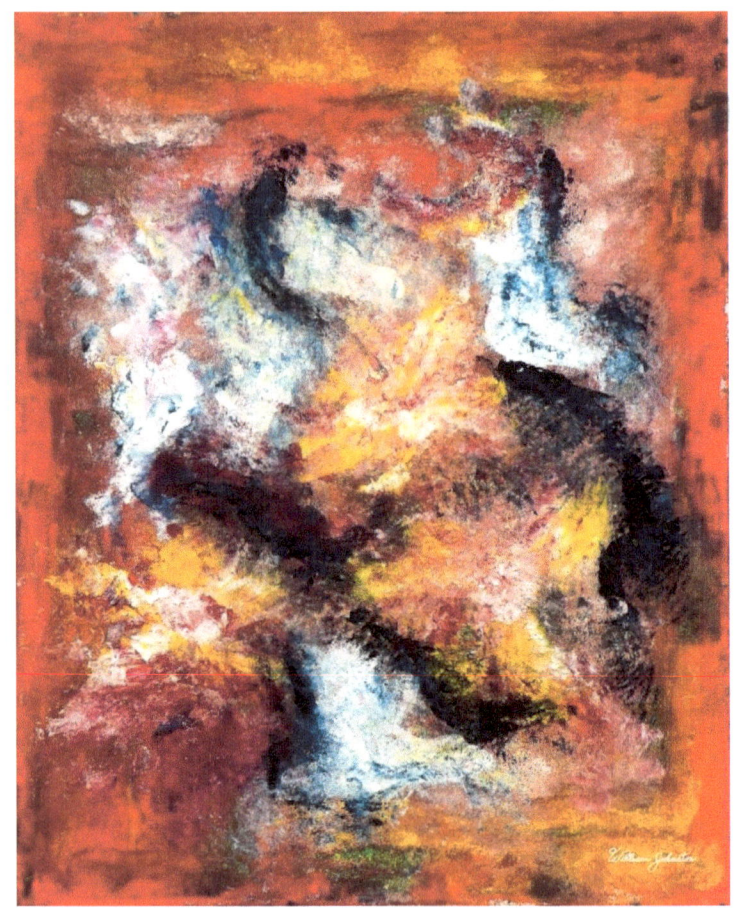

Because of the LORD's great love we are not consumed, for his compassions never fail.

Lamentations 3:22

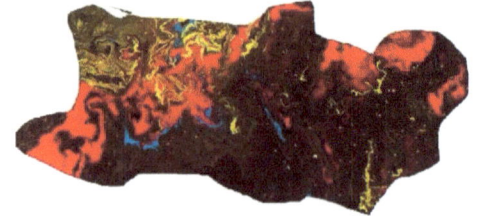

Return and Wait

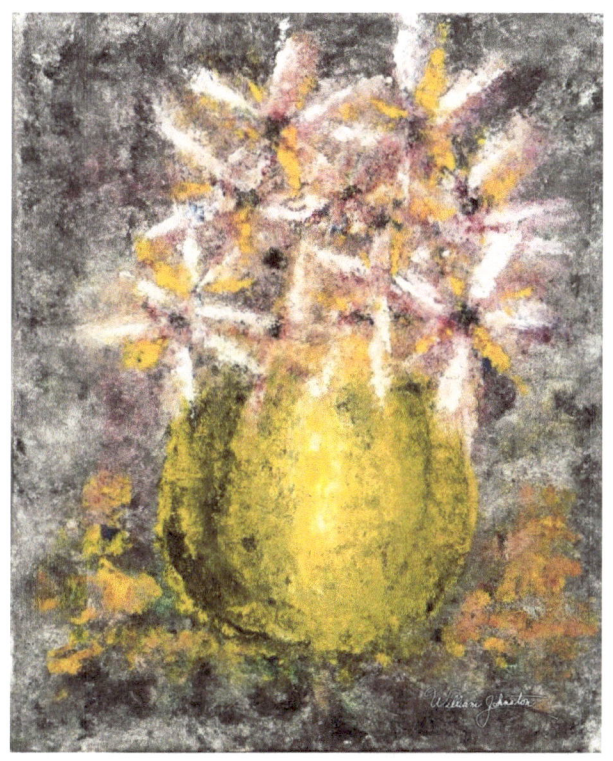

But you must return to your God; maintain love and justice, and wait for your God always.

Hosea 12:6

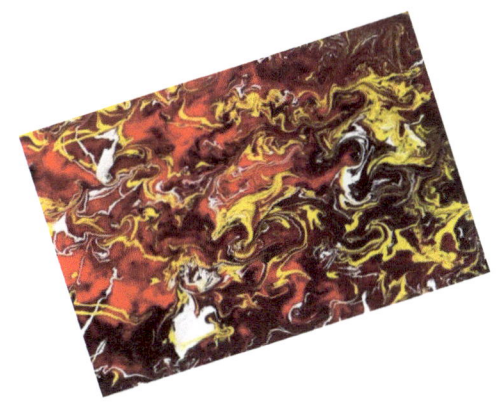

Walk Humbly With Your God

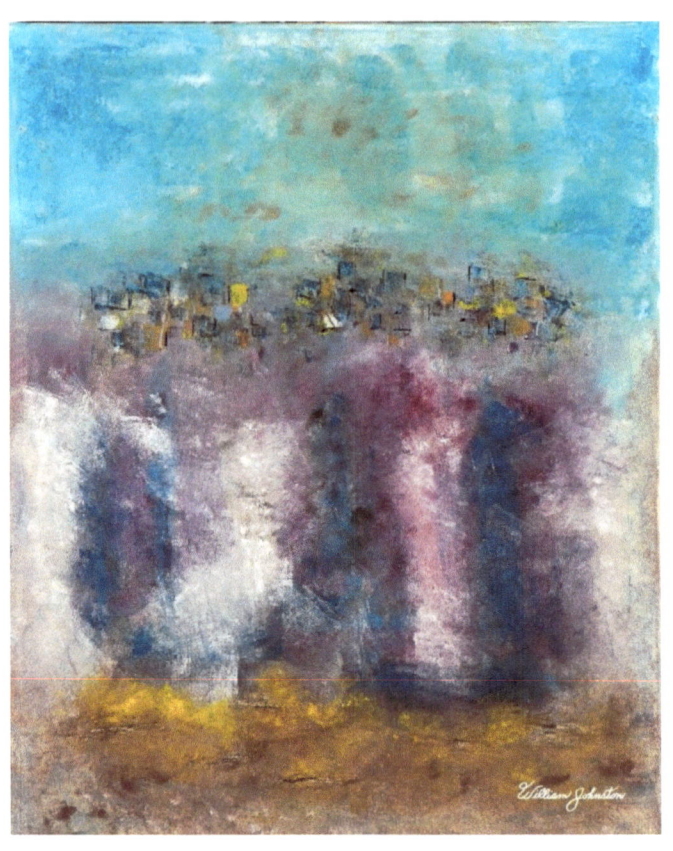

He has showed you, O man, what is good. And what does the LORD require of you? To act justly and to love mercy and to walk humbly with your God.

Micah 6:8

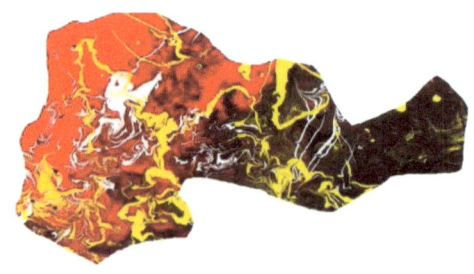

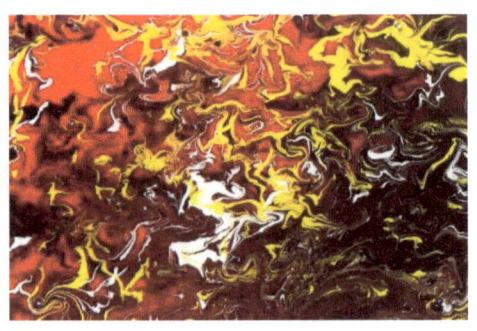

He Is Mighty

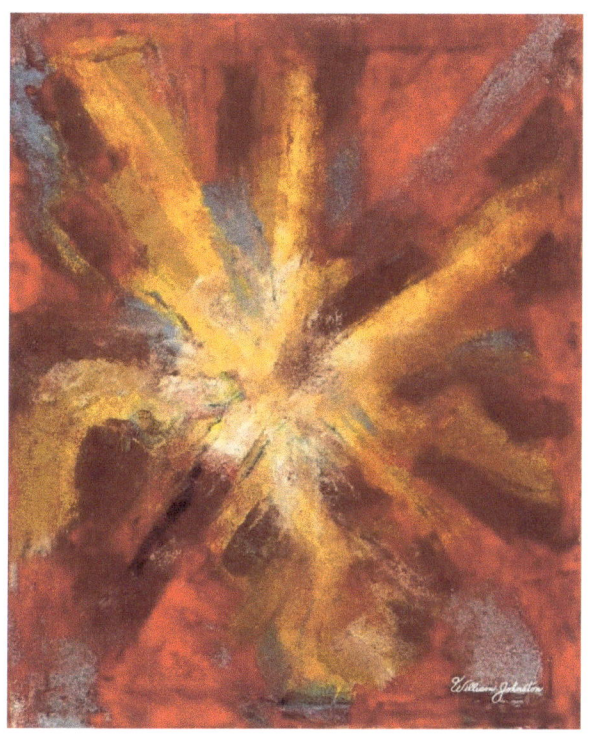

The LORD your God is with you, he is mighty to save. He will take great delight in you, he will quiet you with his love, he will rejoice over you with singing.

Zephaniah 3:17

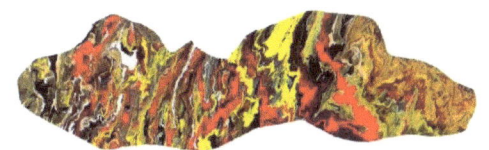

Two Masters

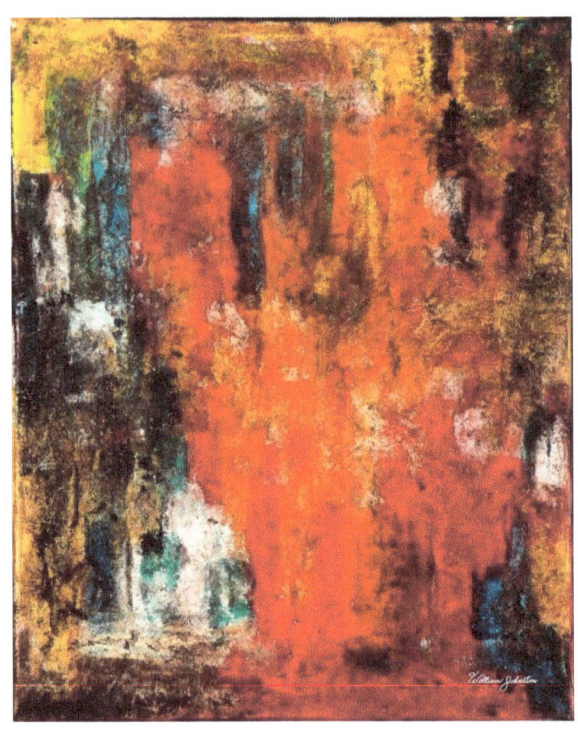

No one can serve two masters. Either he will hate the one and love the other, or he will be devoted to the one and despise the other. You cannot serve both God and Money. Matthew 6:24

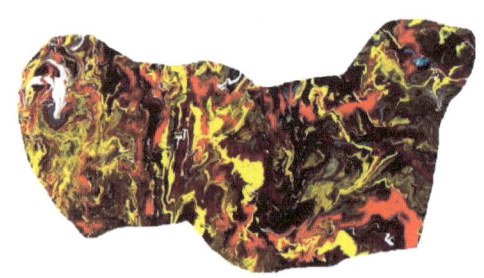

The Greatest Commandment

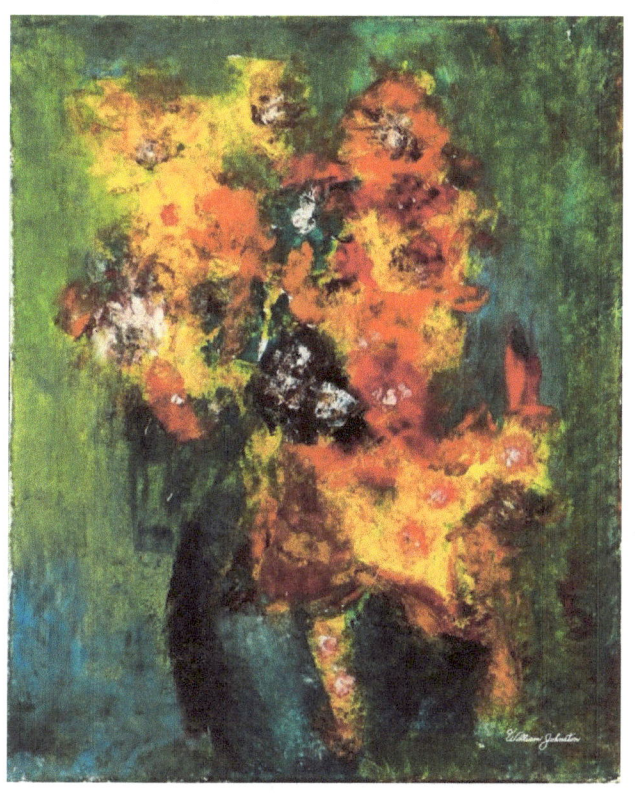

Teacher, which is the greatest commandment in the Law? Jesus replied: 'Love the Lord your God with all your heart and with all your soul and with all your mind.' This is the first and greatest commandment. And the second is like it: 'Love your neighbor as yourself.' All the Law and the Prophets hang on these two commandments. Matthew 22:36-40

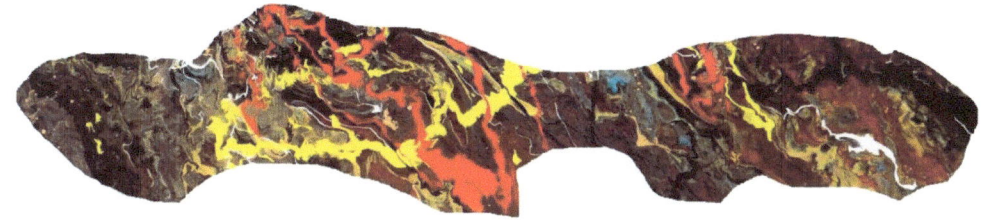

Others

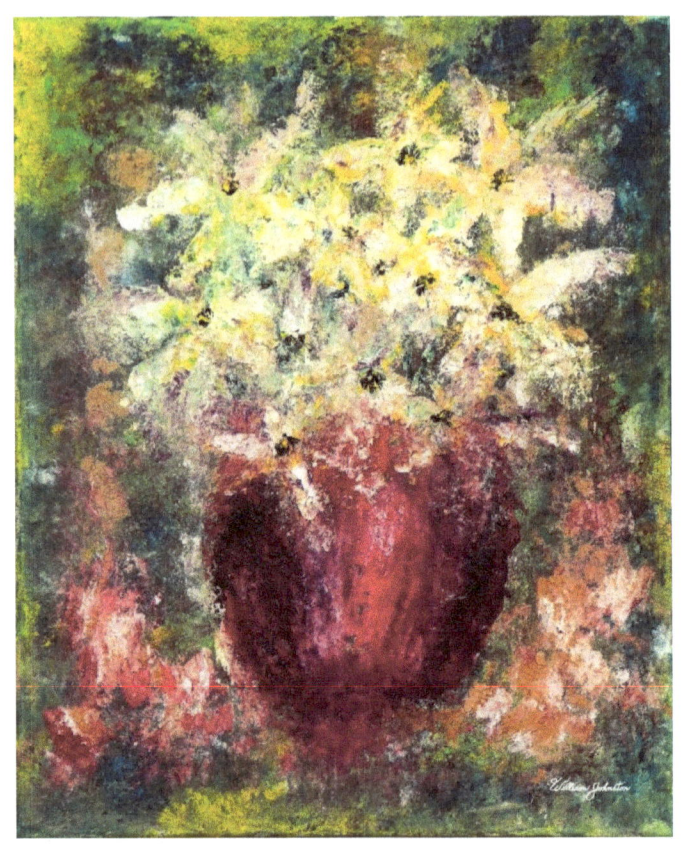

Do to others as you would have them do to you.   Luke 6:31-36

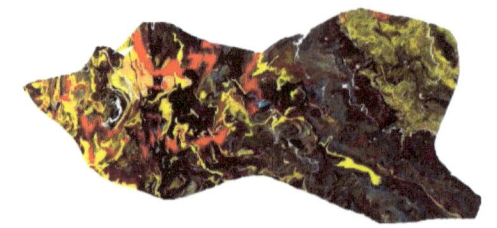

God's Love

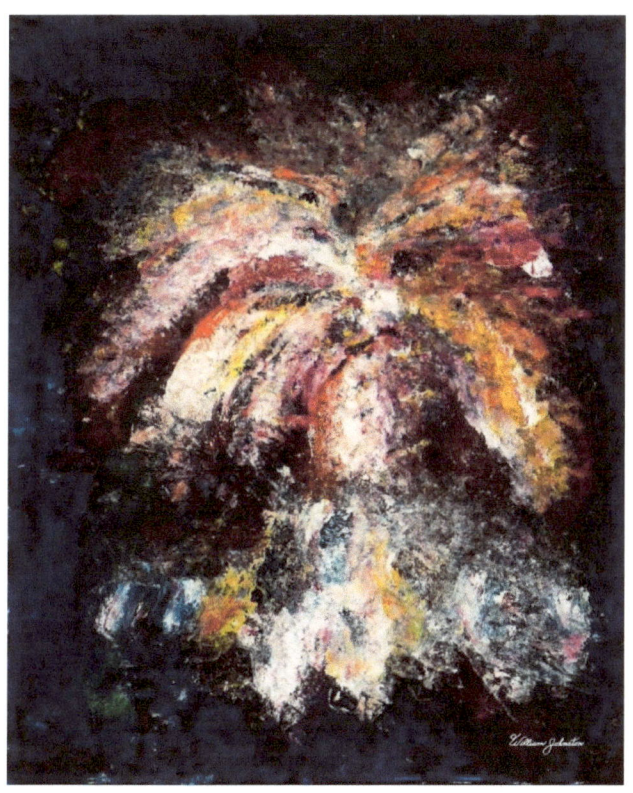

For God so loved the world that he gave his one and only Son, that whoever believes in him shall not perish but have eternal life. John 3:16

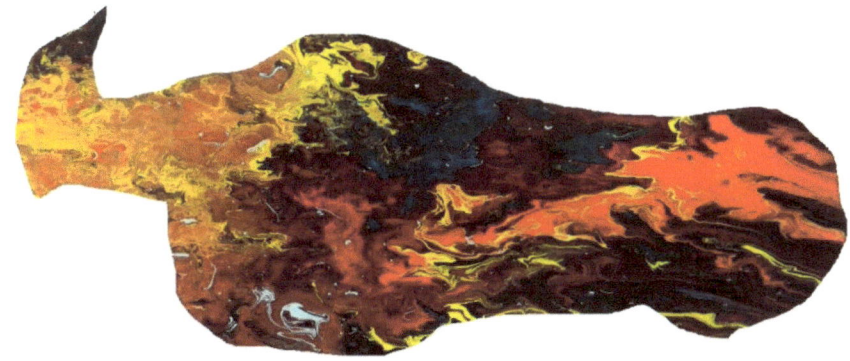

The Book Of Law

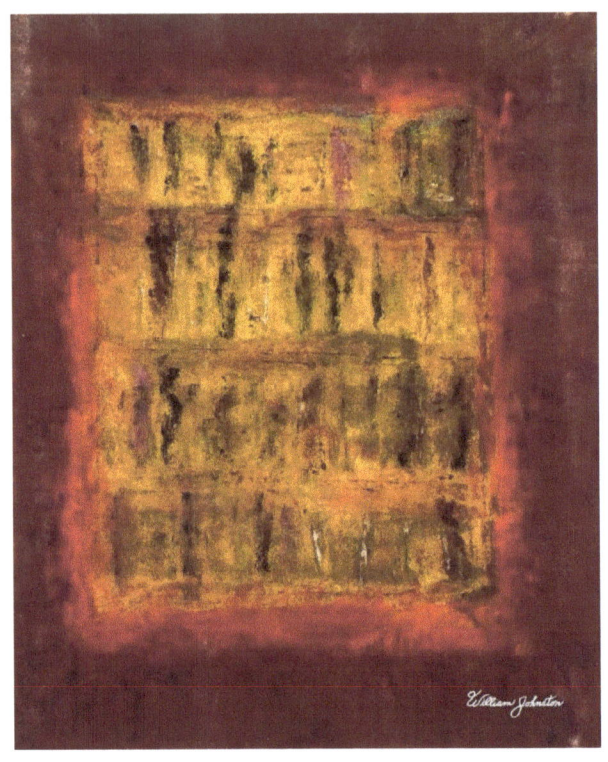

The man who loves his life will lose it, while the man who hates his life in this world will keep it for eternal life. John 12:25

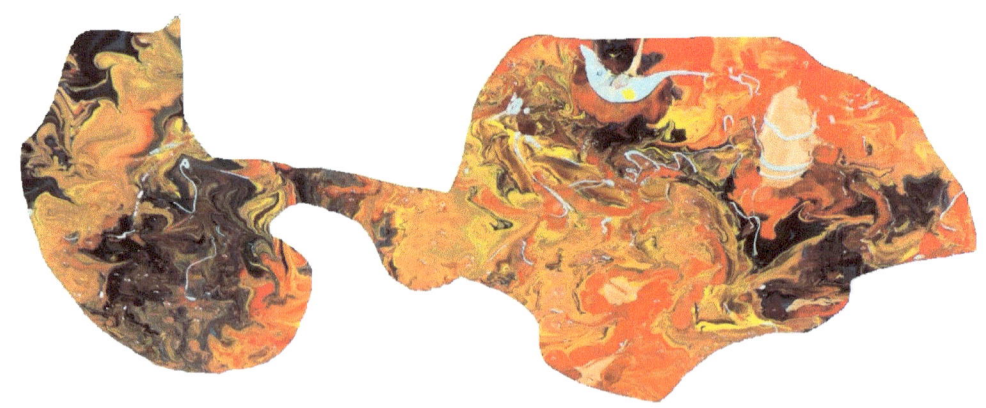

Passover Feast

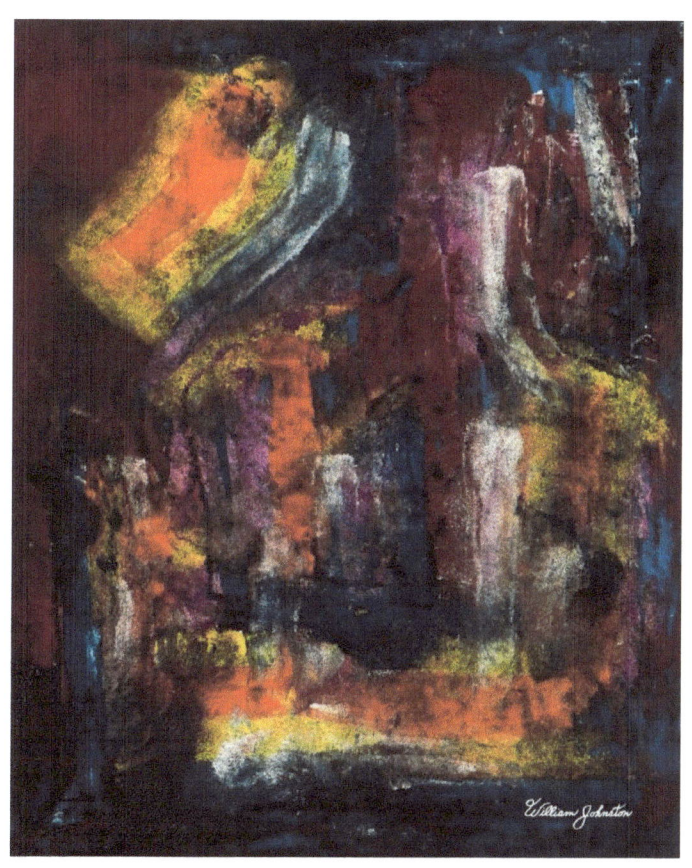

A new command I give you: Love one another. As I have loved you, so you must love one another. By this all men will know that you are my disciples, if you love one another.   John 13:34-35

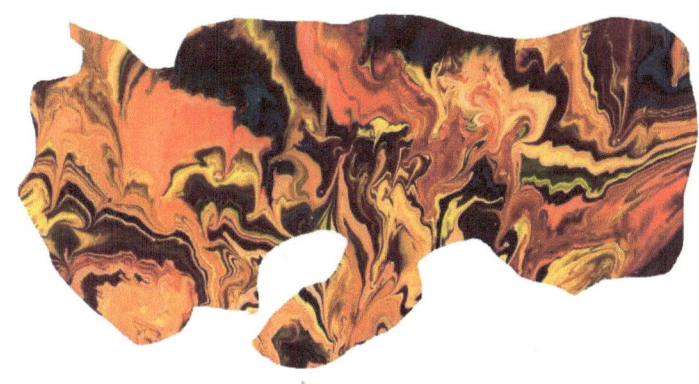

If You Love Me

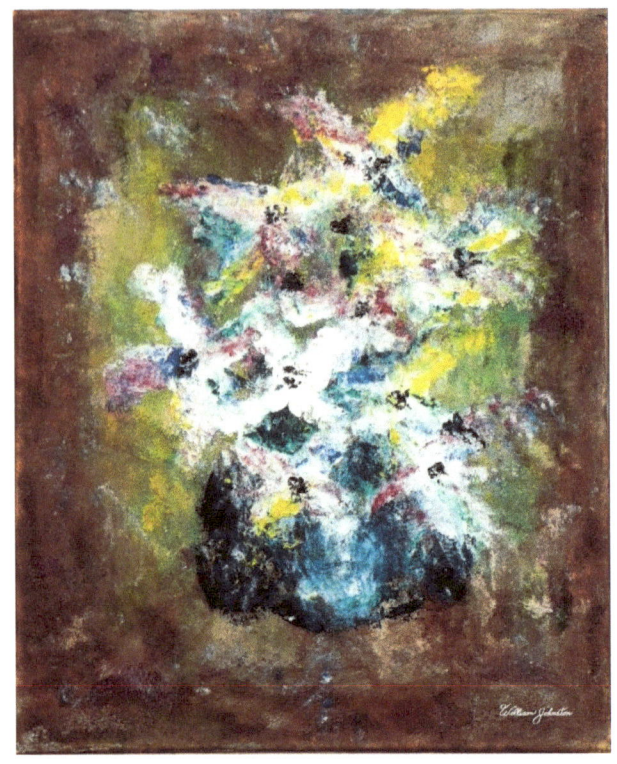

If you love me, you will obey what I command. John 14:15

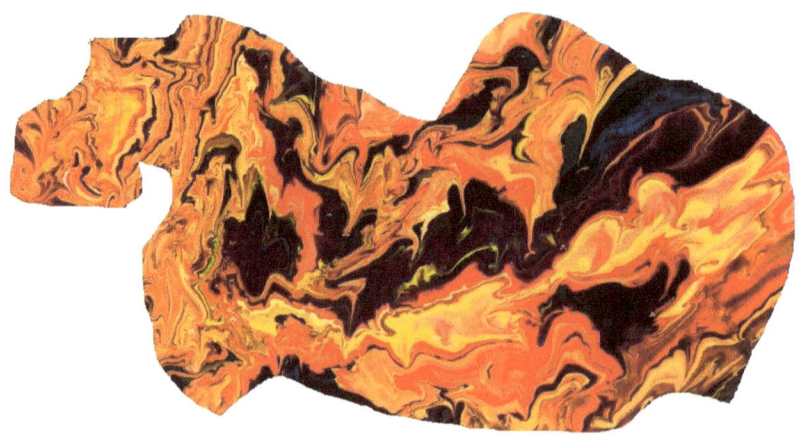

A Father's Love

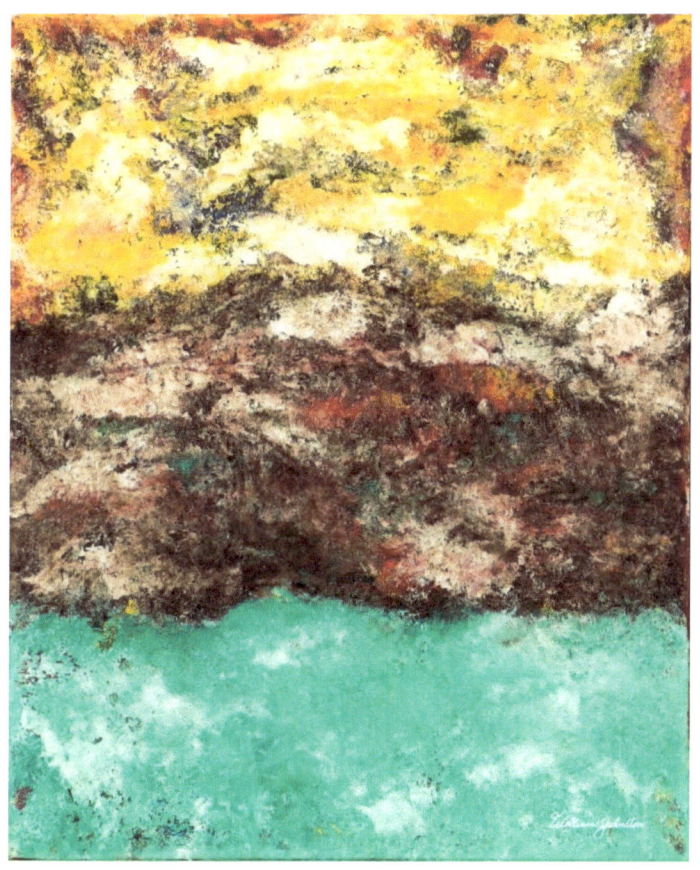

Whoever has my commands and obeys them, he is the one who loves me. He who loves me will be loved by my Father, and I too will love him and show myself to him. John 14:21-25

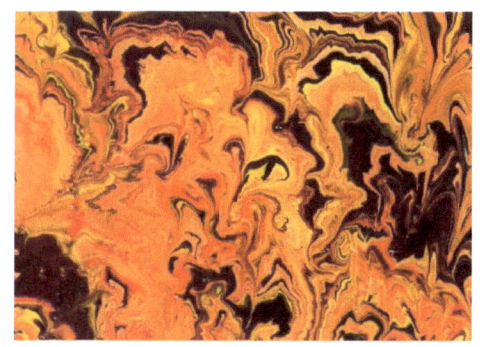

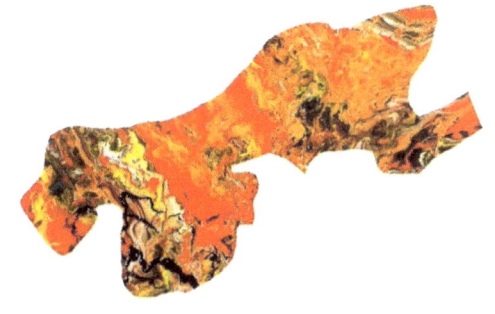

Christ's Joy

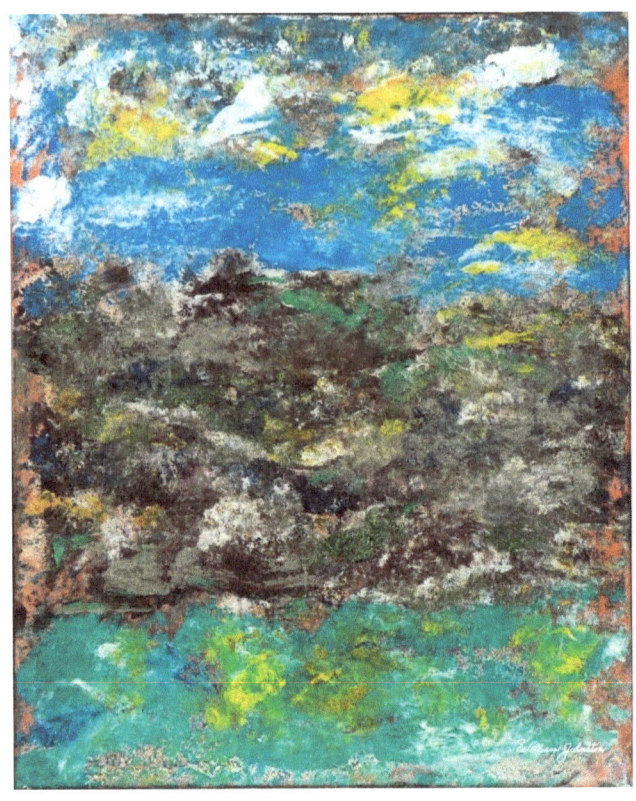

As the Father has loved me, so have I loved you. Now remain in my love. If you obey my commands, you will remain in my love, just as I have obeyed my Father's commands and remain in his love. I have told you this so that my joy may be in you and that your joy may be complete. My command is this: Love each other as I have loved you. Greater love has no one than this, that he lay down his life for his friends.

John 15:9-13

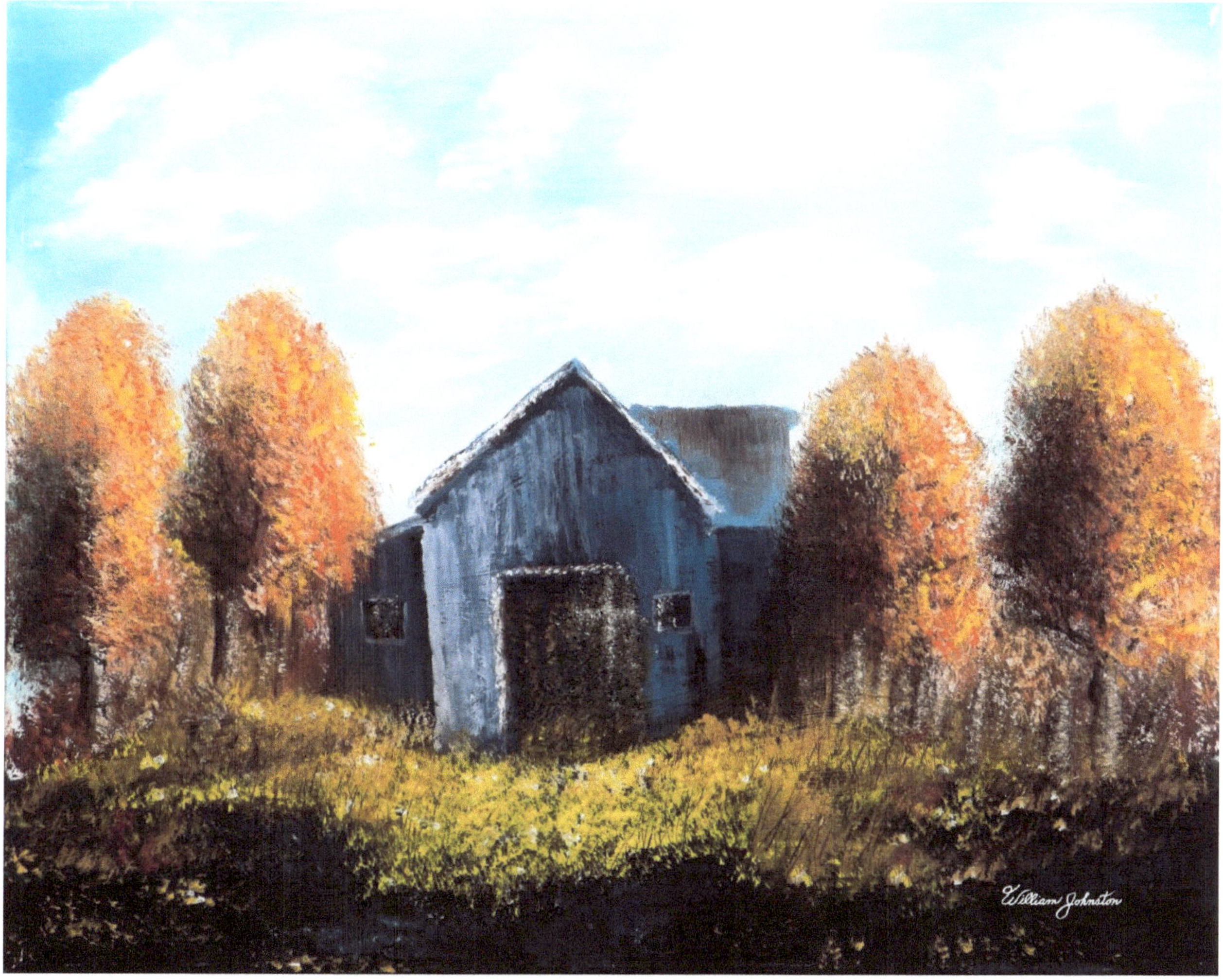

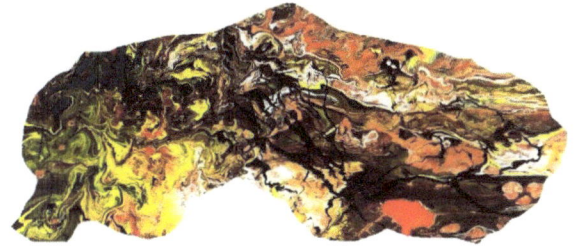

Delight yourself in the LORD and he will give you the desires of your heart.
Psalms 37:4

Heaven's Gate

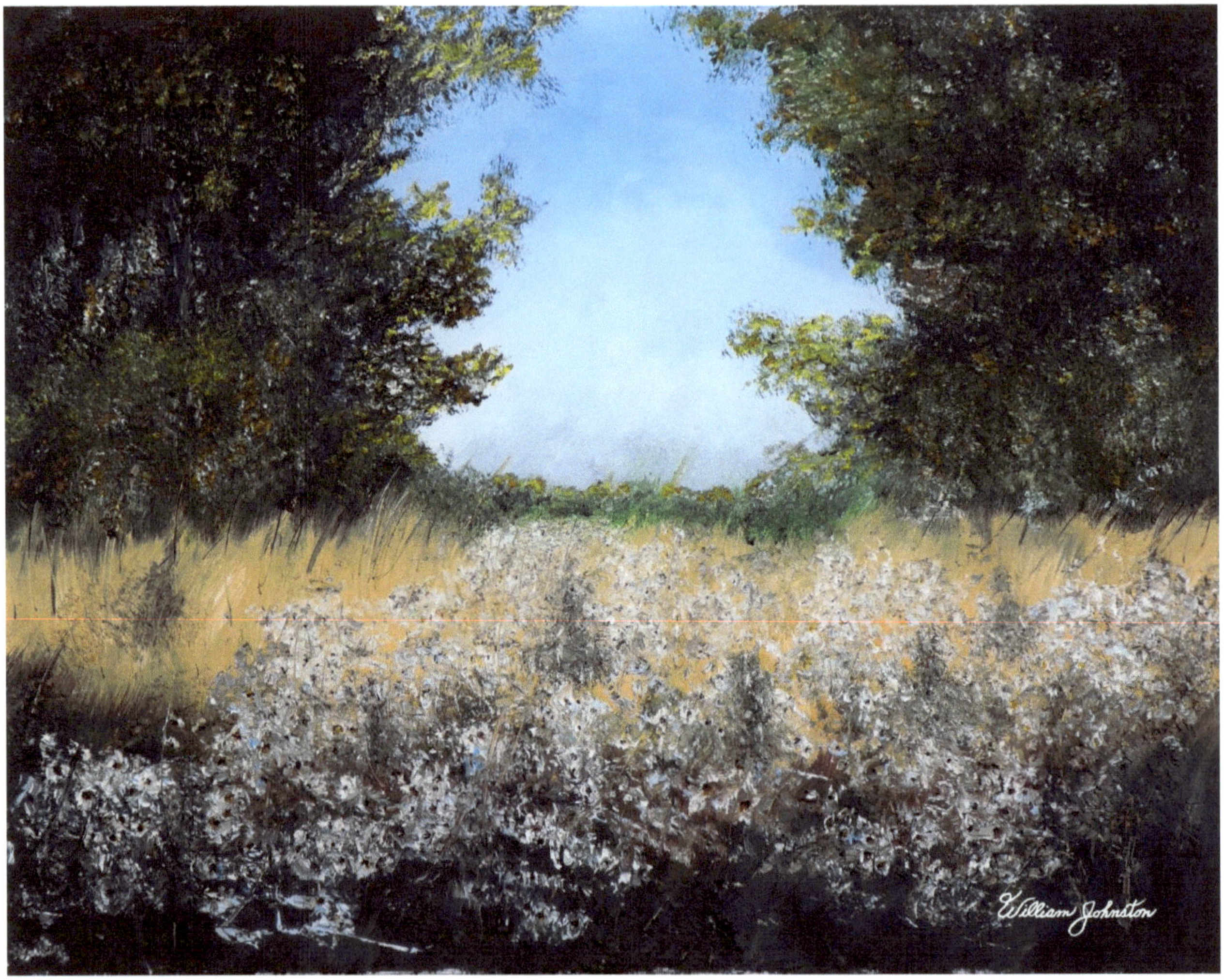

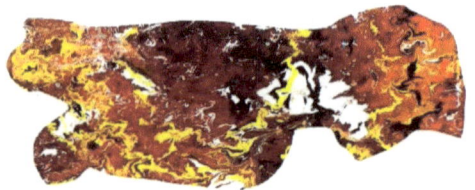

What good will it be for a man if he gains the whole world, yet forfeits his soul? Or what can a man give in exchange for his soul?   *Matthew 16:26*

Heaven

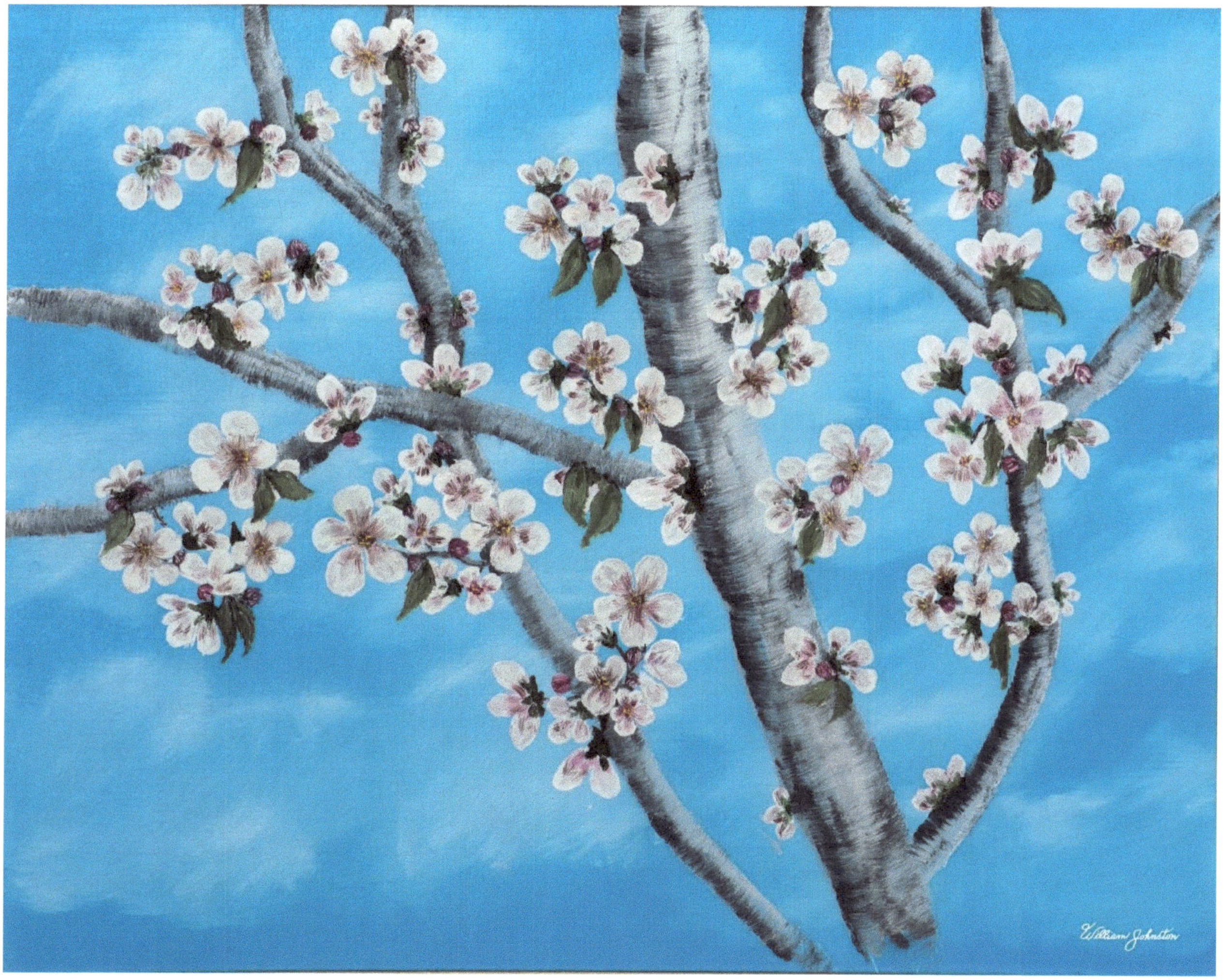

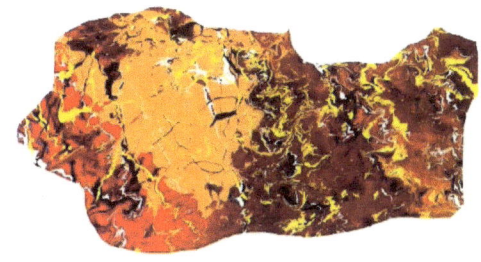

Jesus answered, "I am the way and the truth and the life. No one comes to the Father except through me. John 14:6

Sea at Sunset

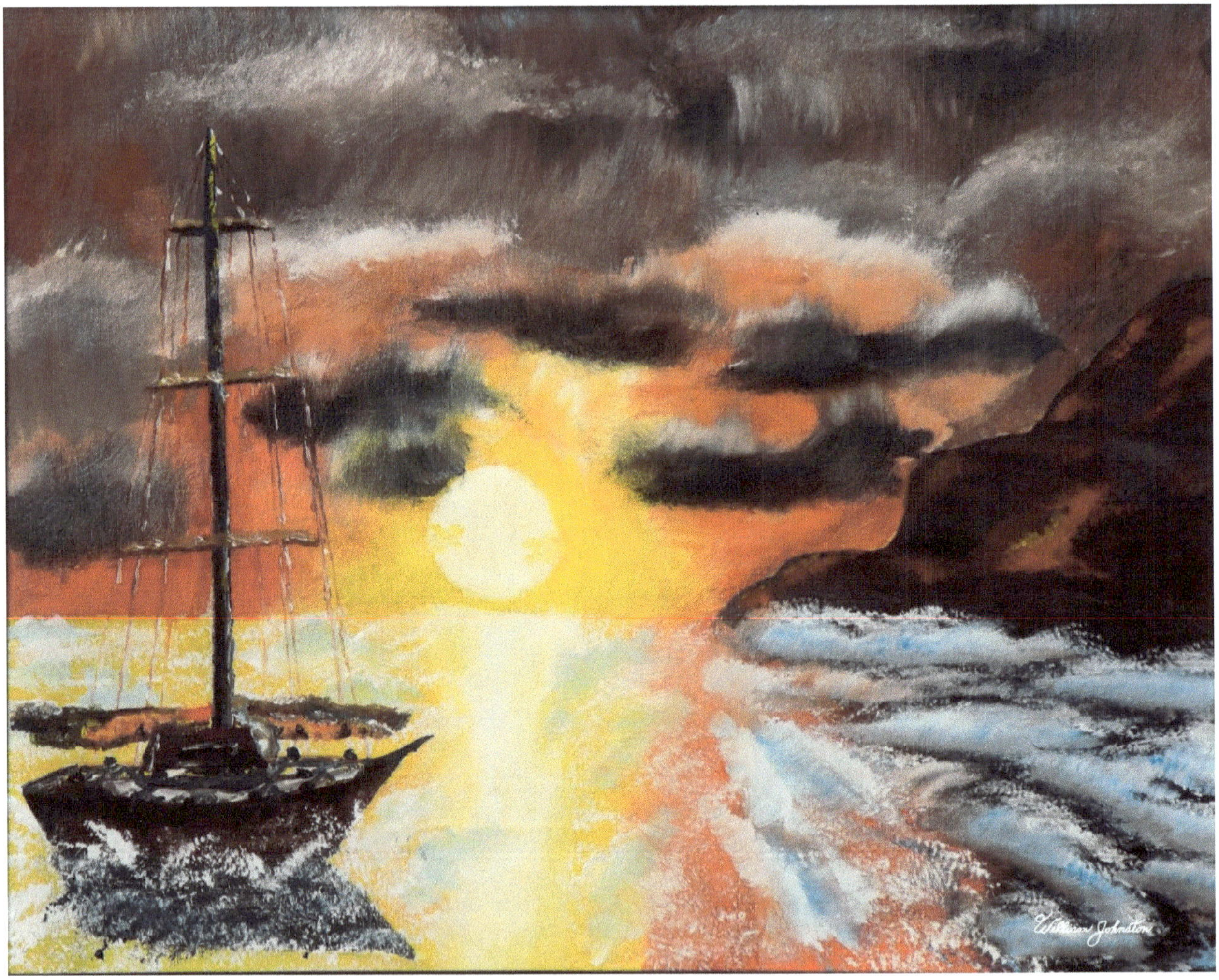

And without faith it is impossible to please God, because anyone who comes to him must believe that he exists and that he rewards those who earnestly seek him. Hebrews 11:6

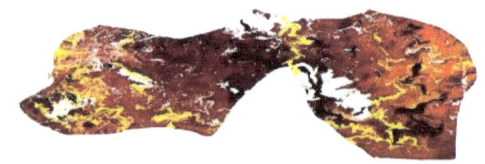

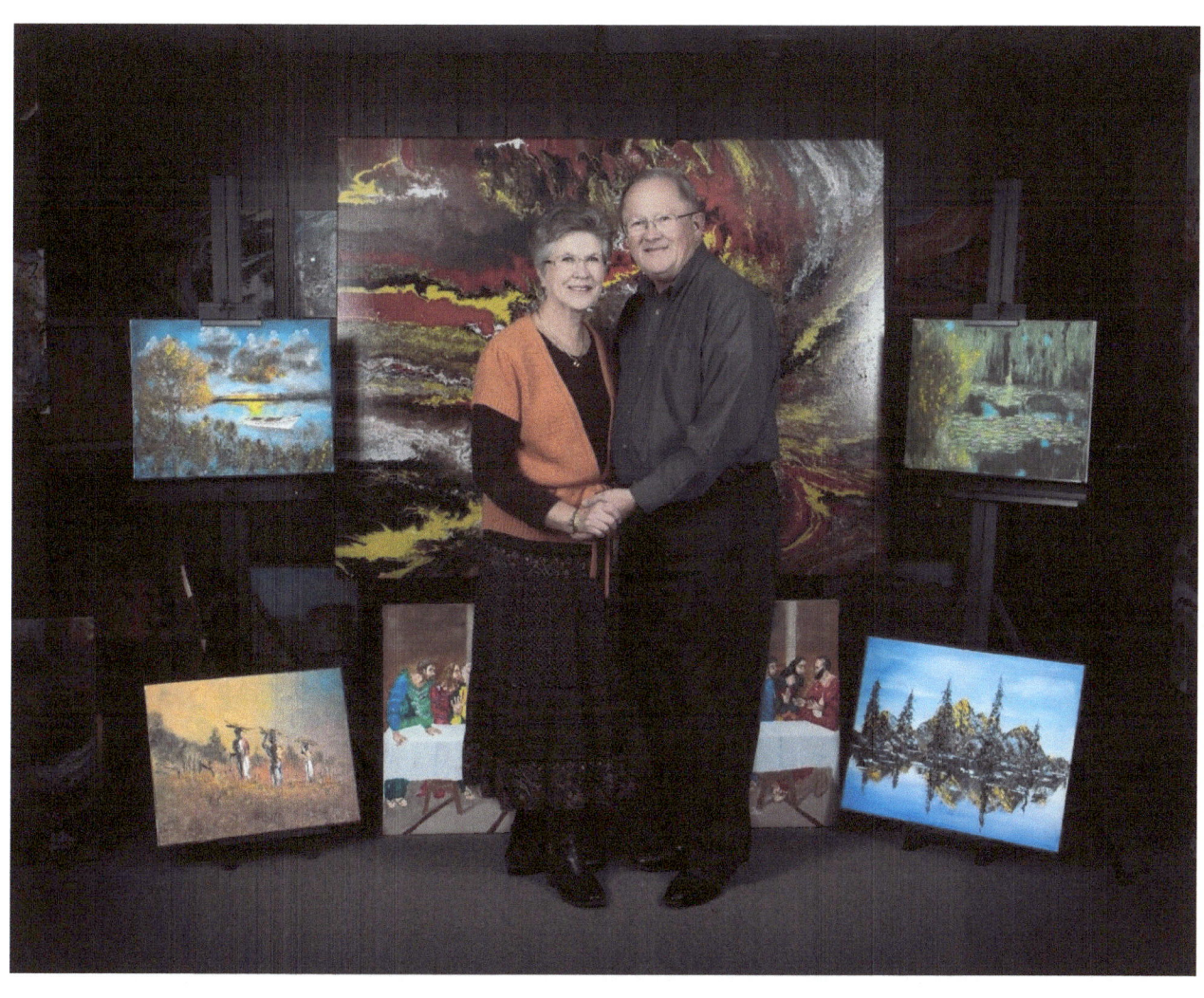

William and Janice Johnston

May the Lord bless you and keep you and may 'The Seeds of His Love' be

a light unto your path that leads you home.

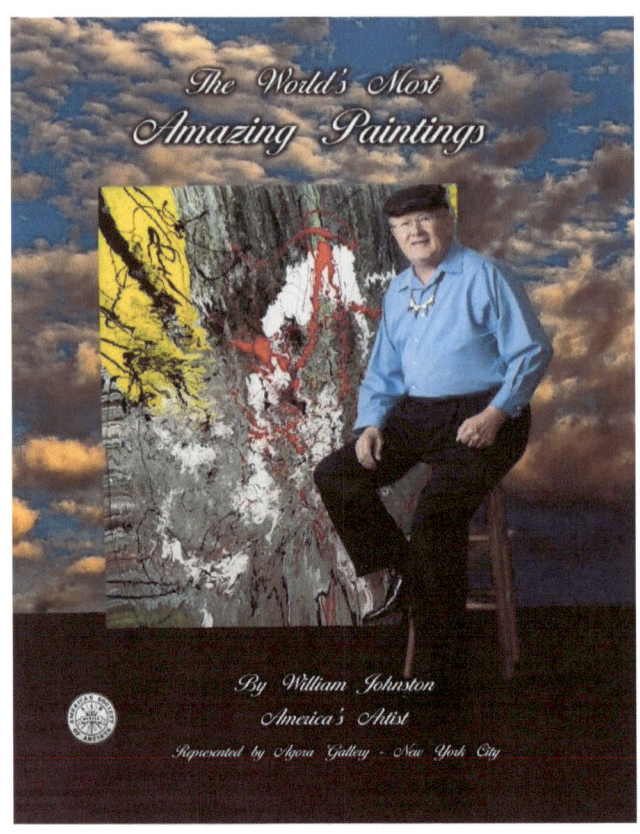

Artist William Johnston

wrjart@yahoo.com – www.wrjart.com

Books and reviews are available at www.amazon.com

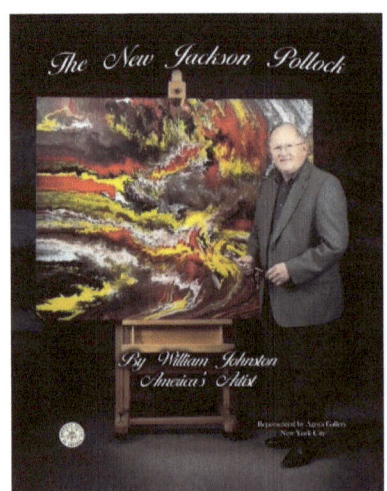
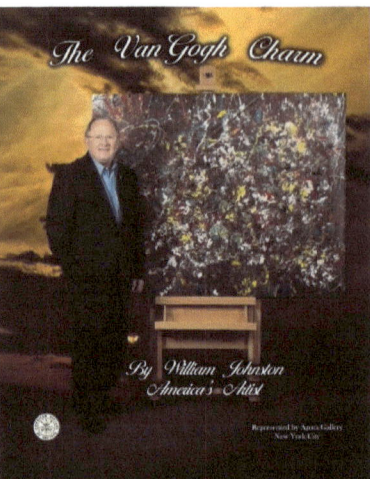
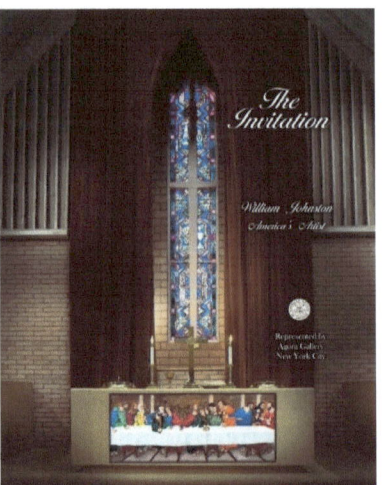